The Magic Life of
MILAREPA

TIBET'S GREAT YOGI

EVA VAN DAM

SHAMBHALA
Boulder
2018

SHAMBHALA PUBLICATIONS, INC.
4720 Walnut Street
Boulder, Colorado 80301
www.shambhala.com

9 8 7 6 5 4 3 2 1

First Edition
Printed in the United States of America

♾ This edition is printed on acid-free paper that meets
the American National Standards Institute Z39.48 Standard.
♻ Shambhala Publications makes every effort to print on recycled paper.
For more information please visit www.shambhala.com.

Shambhala Publications is distributed worldwide by
Penguin Random House, Inc., and its subsidiaries

The Library of Congress catalogues the original edition of this book as follows:
Dam, Eva van
The Magic life of Milarepa, Tibet's great yogi / Eva van Dam
p. cm.
ISBN 9780877734734 (1991 pbk. edition)
ISBN 9781611805260 (2018 pbk. edition)
1. Mi-la-ras-pa, (1040–1123—Comic books, strips, etc.
PN6727.D26M34 1991   89-4z3321
741.5'973—dc20 CIP

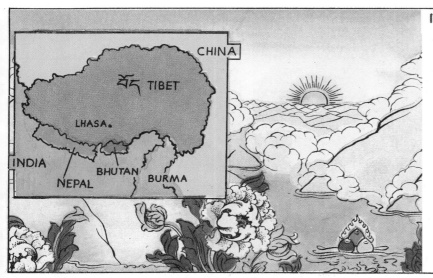

IT IS THE YEAR 1050, THE TIBETAN MIDDLE AGES.
AFTER A LONG REIGN BY BON-PO CLANS,
WHO RULED THE LAND FROM LHASA,
THE IMPERIAL SYSTEM HAD COMPLETELY
DISINTEGRATED. THE COUNTRY WAS
BROKEN UP INTO MANY SMALL PARTS,
RULED BY A NEW FEUDAL NOBILITY, EACH
WITH ITS OWN FORTRESS.
AFTER TWO HUNDRED YEARS OF PERSECU-
TION OF BUDDHISM, PRACTICES OF MAGIC
AND SUPERSTITION, MIXED WITH WHAT WAS
REMEMBERED OF THE TANTRIC TEACHINGS
OF PADMASAMBHAVA, WERE THE ONLY
FORM IN WHICH RELIGION EXISTED.
THE ARRIVAL OF THE FAMOUS MASTER
ATISHA IN 1042 AND OTHER LEARNED
MONKS FROM INDIA WAS THE START
OF THE RENAISSANCE OF BUDDHISM
IN TIBET. A GREAT PERIOD IN TIBETAN
HISTORY BEGAN.

KYA NGA TSA.	MILAREPA'S BIRTHPLACE.
KU-LUNG.	WHERE HE LEARNED TO CAUSE DEATH BY MAGIC.
TROWO-LUNG.	MARPA'S VILLAGE.
NYA-NANG.	STOMACH-LIKE CAVE.
LANGDA.	VILLAGE WHERE MILAREPA WAS SEEN FLYING.
TINGRI.	AREA WITH MANY CAVES OF MILAREPA.

CENTRAL AND SOUTHERN TIBET

A VILLAGE IN TIBET.

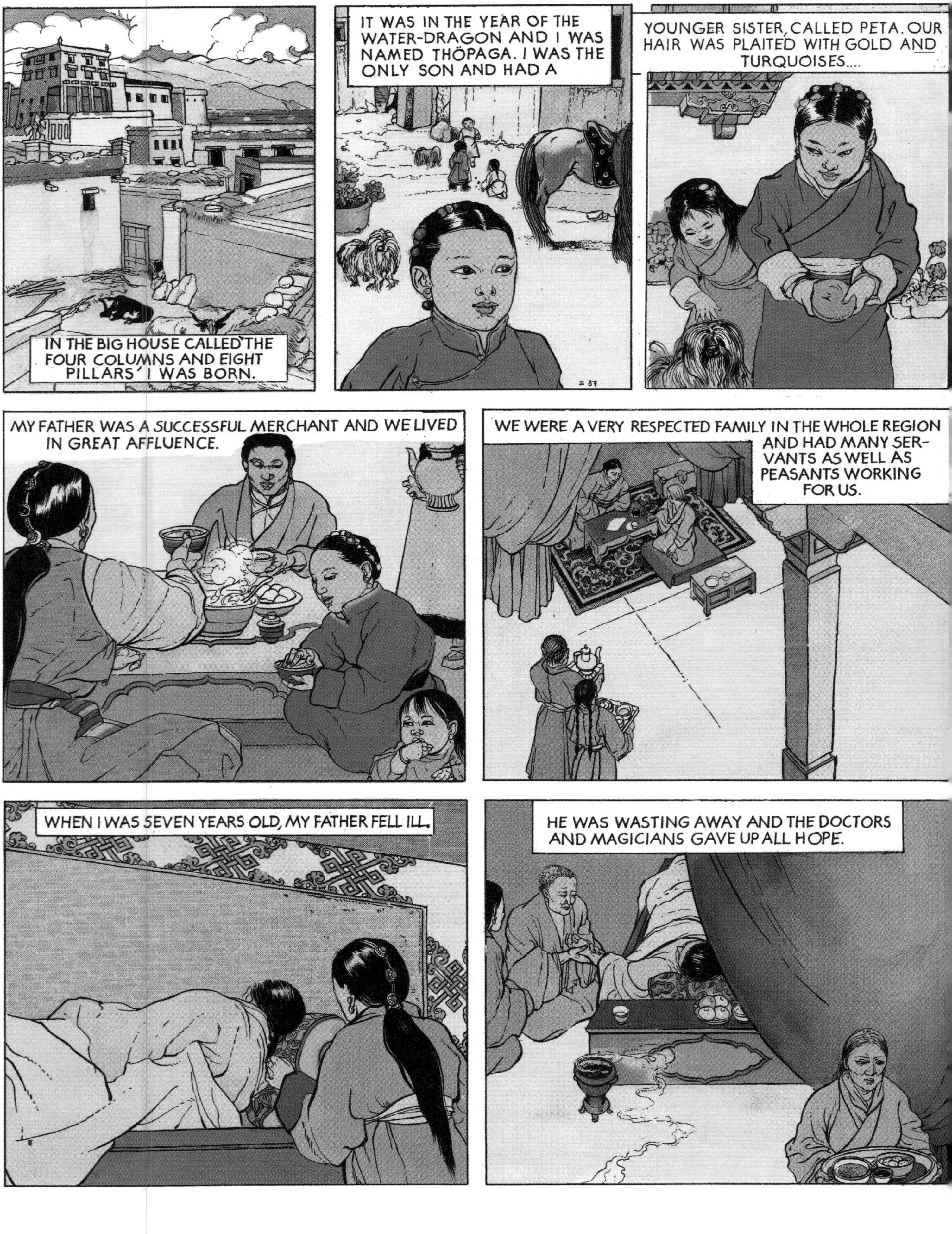
IN THE BIG HOUSE CALLED 'THE FOUR COLUMNS AND EIGHT PILLARS' I WAS BORN.
IT WAS IN THE YEAR OF THE WATER-DRAGON AND I WAS NAMED THÖPAGA. I WAS THE ONLY SON AND HAD A
YOUNGER SISTER, CALLED PETA. OUR HAIR WAS PLAITED WITH GOLD AND TURQUOISES....
MY FATHER WAS A *SUCCESSFUL* MERCHANT AND WE LIVED IN GREAT AFFLUENCE.
WE WERE A VERY RESPECTED FAMILY IN THE WHOLE REGION AND HAD MANY SERVANTS AS WELL AS PEASANTS WORKING FOR US.
WHEN I WAS SEVEN YEARS OLD, MY FATHER FELL ILL.
HE WAS WASTING AWAY AND THE DOCTORS AND MAGICIANS GAVE UP ALL HOPE.

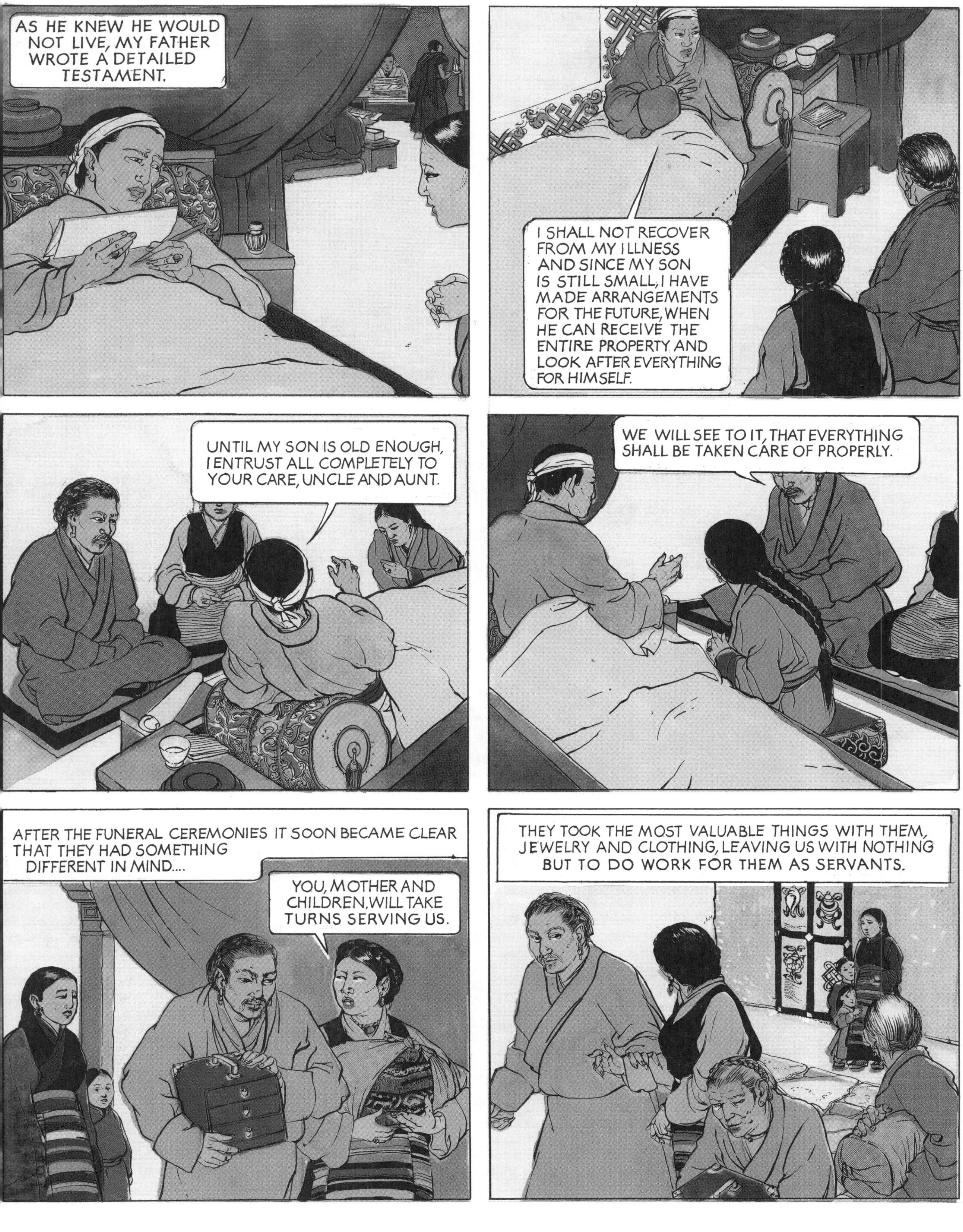
AS HE KNEW HE WOULD NOT LIVE, MY FATHER WROTE A DETAILED TESTAMENT.
I SHALL NOT RECOVER FROM MY ILLNESS AND SINCE MY SON IS STILL SMALL, I HAVE MADE ARRANGEMENTS FOR THE FUTURE, WHEN HE CAN RECEIVE THE ENTIRE PROPERTY AND LOOK AFTER EVERYTHING FOR HIMSELF.
UNTIL MY SON IS OLD ENOUGH, I ENTRUST ALL COMPLETELY TO YOUR CARE, UNCLE AND AUNT.
WE WILL SEE TO IT, THAT EVERYTHING SHALL BE TAKEN CARE OF PROPERLY.
AFTER THE FUNERAL CEREMONIES IT SOON BECAME CLEAR THAT THEY HAD SOMETHING DIFFERENT IN MIND....
YOU, MOTHER AND CHILDREN, WILL TAKE TURNS SERVING US.
THEY TOOK THE MOST VALUABLE THINGS WITH THEM, JEWELRY AND CLOTHING, LEAVING US WITH NOTHING BUT TO DO WORK FOR THEM AS SERVANTS.

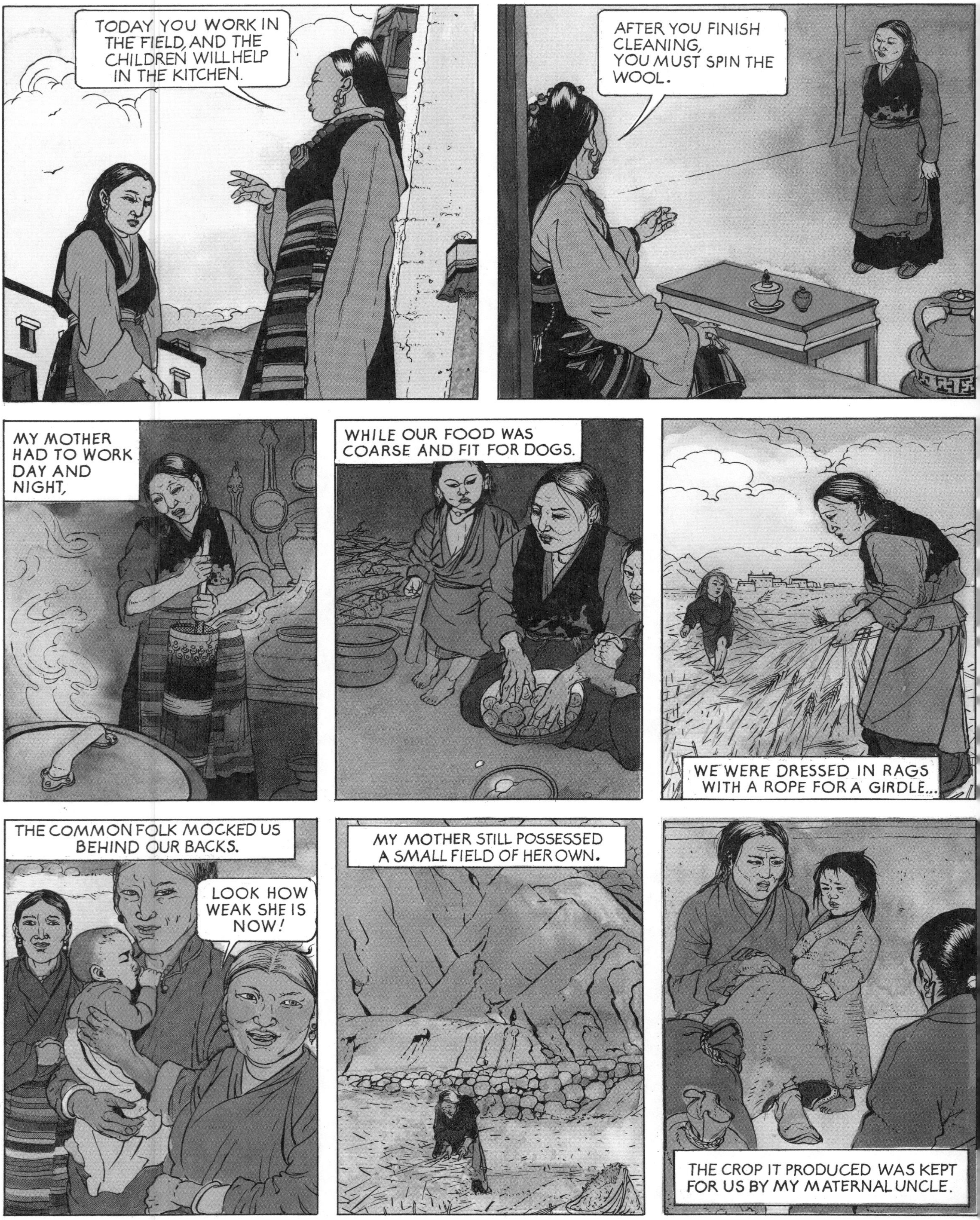
TODAY YOU WORK IN THE FIELD, AND THE CHILDREN WILL HELP IN THE KITCHEN.
AFTER YOU FINISH CLEANING, YOU MUST SPIN THE WOOL.
MY MOTHER HAD TO WORK DAY AND NIGHT,
WHILE OUR FOOD WAS COARSE AND FIT FOR DOGS.
WE WERE DRESSED IN RAGS WITH A ROPE FOR A GIRDLE...
THE COMMON FOLK MOCKED US BEHIND OUR BACKS.
LOOK HOW WEAK SHE IS NOW!
MY MOTHER STILL POSSESSED A SMALL FIELD OF HER OWN.
THE CROP IT PRODUCED WAS KEPT FOR US BY MY MATERNAL UNCLE.

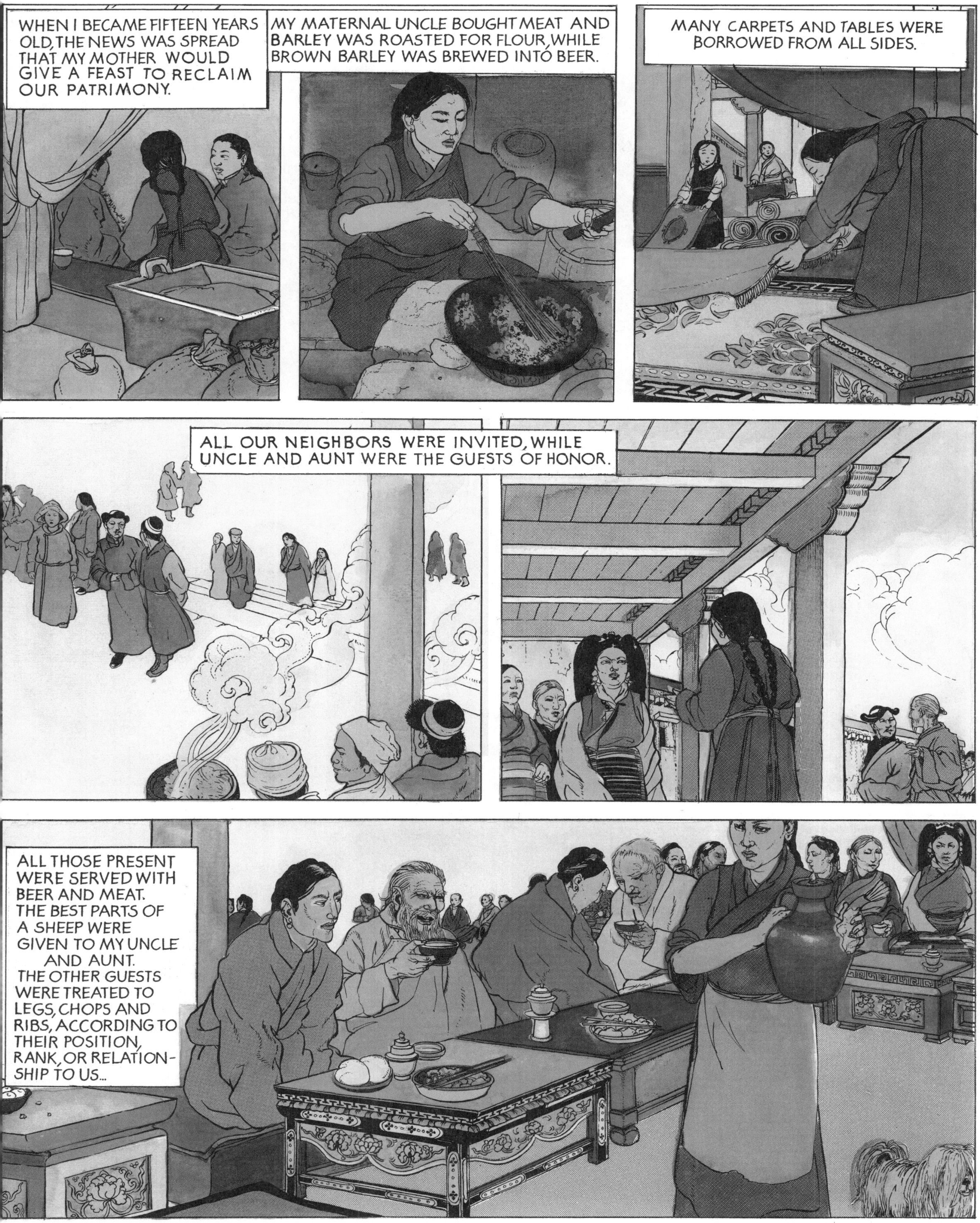
WHEN I BECAME FIFTEEN YEARS OLD, THE NEWS WAS SPREAD THAT MY MOTHER WOULD GIVE A FEAST TO RECLAIM OUR PATRIMONY.
MY MATERNAL UNCLE BOUGHT MEAT AND BARLEY WAS ROASTED FOR FLOUR, WHILE BROWN BARLEY WAS BREWED INTO BEER.
MANY CARPETS AND TABLES WERE BORROWED FROM ALL SIDES.
ALL OUR NEIGHBORS WERE INVITED, WHILE UNCLE AND AUNT WERE THE GUESTS OF HONOR.
ALL THOSE PRESENT WERE SERVED WITH BEER AND MEAT. THE BEST PARTS OF A SHEEP WERE GIVEN TO MY UNCLE AND AUNT. THE OTHER GUESTS WERE TREATED TO LEGS, CHOPS AND RIBS, ACCORDING TO THEIR POSITION, RANK, OR RELATION-SHIP TO US...

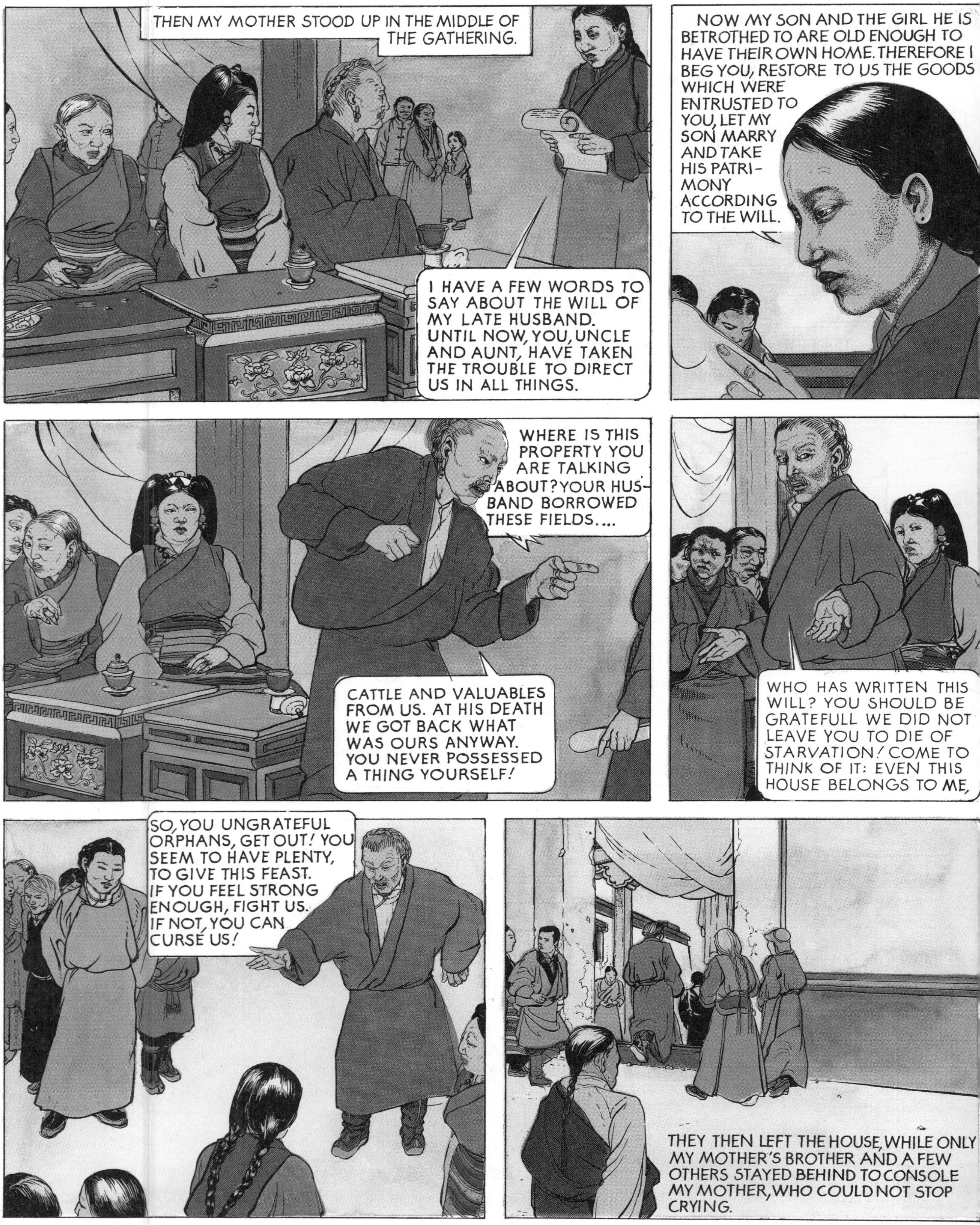
THEN MY MOTHER STOOD UP IN THE MIDDLE OF THE GATHERING.
I HAVE A FEW WORDS TO SAY ABOUT THE WILL OF MY LATE HUSBAND. UNTIL NOW, YOU, UNCLE AND AUNT, HAVE TAKEN THE TROUBLE TO DIRECT US IN ALL THINGS.
NOW MY SON AND THE GIRL HE IS BETROTHED TO ARE OLD ENOUGH TO HAVE THEIR OWN HOME. THEREFORE I BEG YOU, RESTORE TO US THE GOODS WHICH WERE ENTRUSTED TO YOU, LET MY SON MARRY AND TAKE HIS PATRIMONY ACCORDING TO THE WILL.
WHERE IS THIS PROPERTY YOU ARE TALKING ABOUT? YOUR HUSBAND BORROWED THESE FIELDS....
CATTLE AND VALUABLES FROM US. AT HIS DEATH WE GOT BACK WHAT WAS OURS ANYWAY. YOU NEVER POSSESSED A THING YOURSELF!
WHO HAS WRITTEN THIS WILL? YOU SHOULD BE GRATEFULL WE DID NOT LEAVE YOU TO DIE OF STARVATION! COME TO THINK OF IT: EVEN THIS HOUSE BELONGS TO ME,
SO, YOU UNGRATEFUL ORPHANS, GET OUT! YOU SEEM TO HAVE PLENTY, TO GIVE THIS FEAST. IF YOU FEEL STRONG ENOUGH, FIGHT US. IF NOT, YOU CAN CURSE US!
THEY THEN LEFT THE HOUSE, WHILE ONLY MY MOTHER'S BROTHER AND A FEW OTHERS STAYED BEHIND TO CONSOLE MY MOTHER, WHO COULD NOT STOP CRYING.

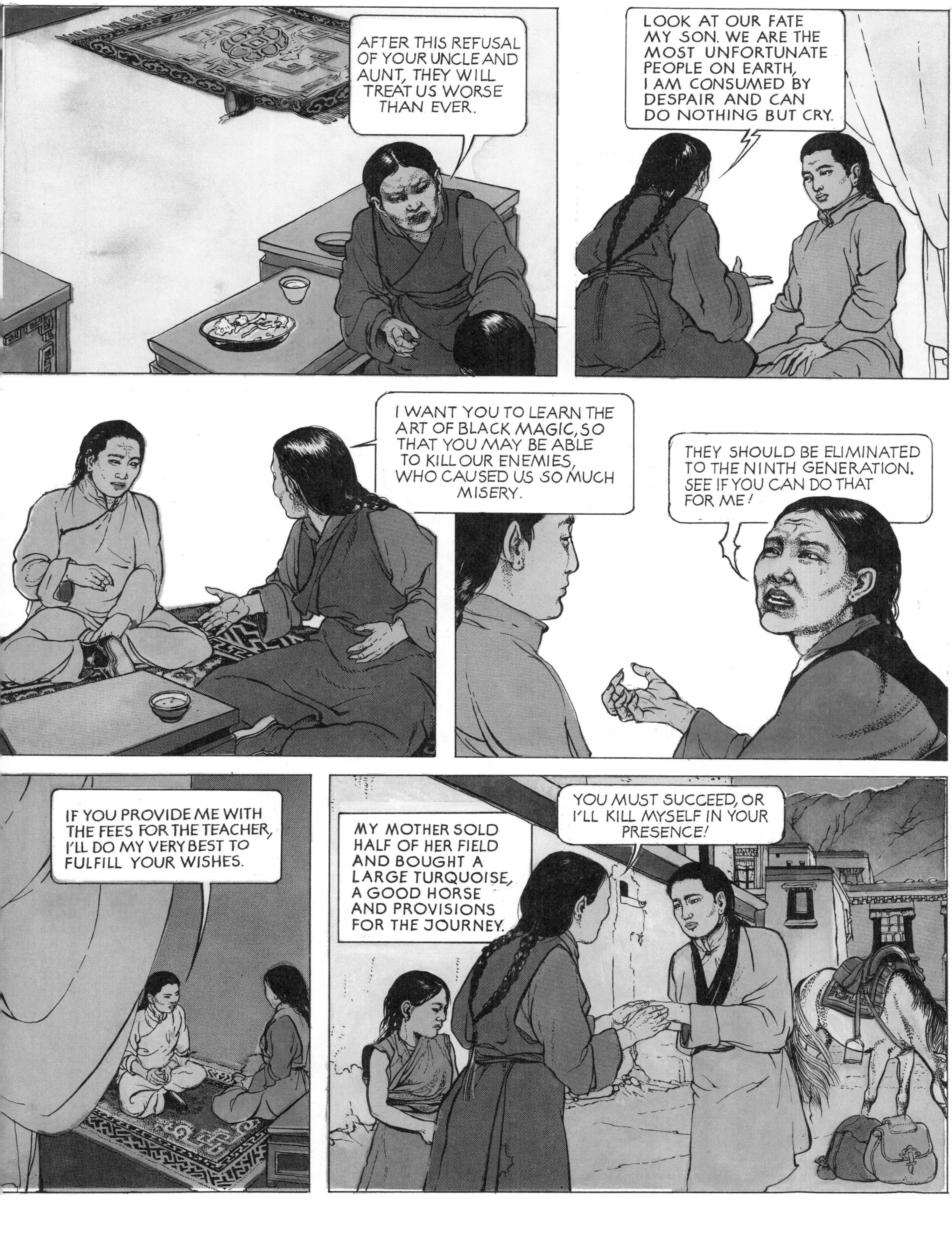
AFTER THIS REFUSAL OF YOUR UNCLE AND AUNT, THEY WILL TREAT US WORSE THAN EVER.
LOOK AT OUR FATE MY SON. WE ARE THE MOST UNFORTUNATE PEOPLE ON EARTH, I AM CONSUMED BY DESPAIR AND CAN DO NOTHING BUT CRY.
I WANT YOU TO LEARN THE ART OF BLACK MAGIC, SO THAT YOU MAY BE ABLE TO KILL OUR ENEMIES, WHO CAUSED US SO MUCH MISERY.
THEY SHOULD BE ELIMINATED TO THE NINTH GENERATION. SEE IF YOU CAN DO THAT FOR ME!
IF YOU PROVIDE ME WITH THE FEES FOR THE TEACHER, I'LL DO MY VERY BEST TO FULFILL YOUR WISHES.
MY MOTHER SOLD HALF OF HER FIELD AND BOUGHT A LARGE TURQUOISE, A GOOD HORSE AND PROVISIONS FOR THE JOURNEY.
YOU MUST SUCCEED, OR I'LL KILL MYSELF IN YOUR PRESENCE!

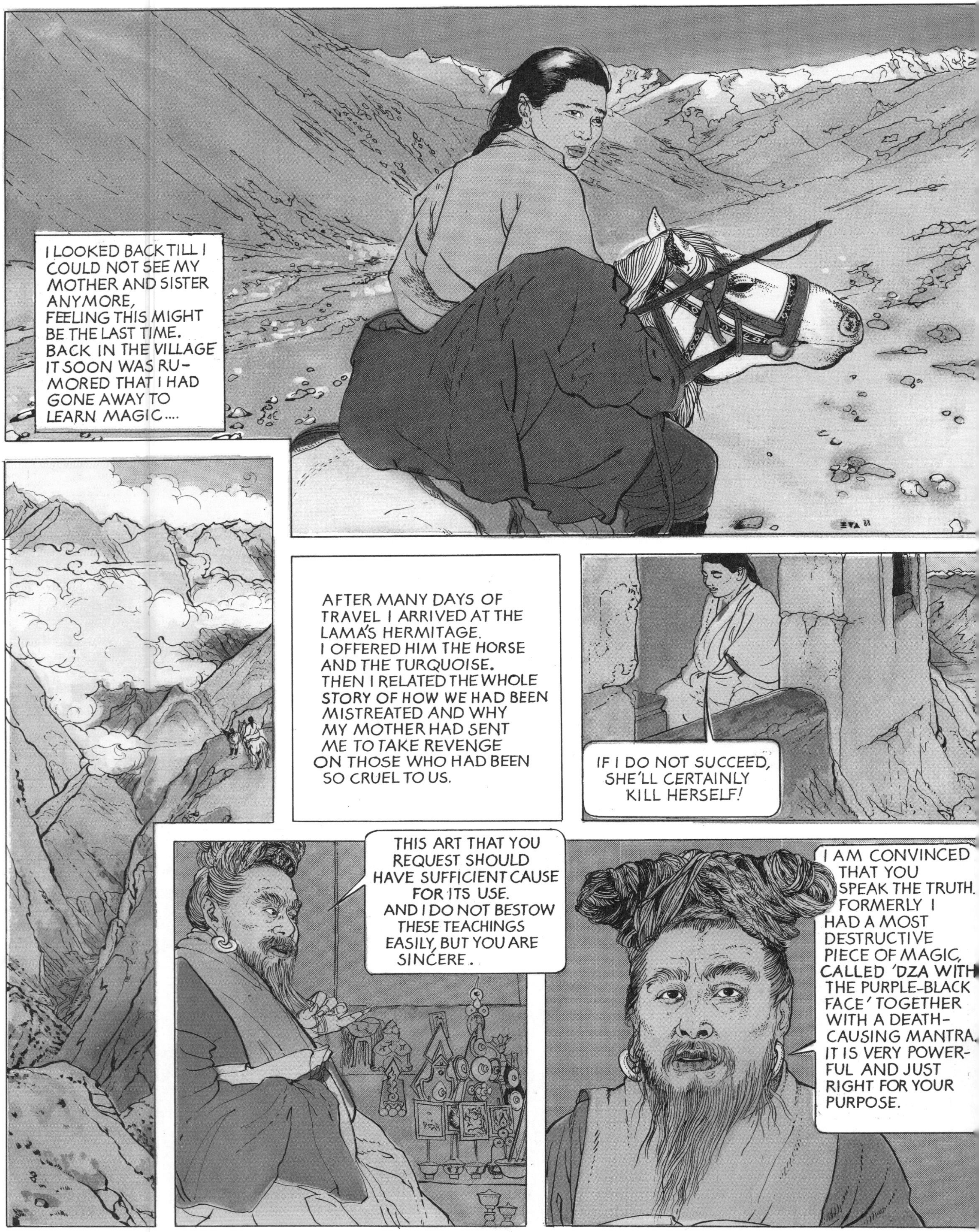
I LOOKED BACK TILL I COULD NOT SEE MY MOTHER AND SISTER ANYMORE, FEELING THIS MIGHT BE THE LAST TIME. BACK IN THE VILLAGE IT SOON WAS RUMORED THAT I HAD GONE AWAY TO LEARN MAGIC....
AFTER MANY DAYS OF TRAVEL I ARRIVED AT THE LAMA'S HERMITAGE. I OFFERED HIM THE HORSE AND THE TURQUOISE. THEN I RELATED THE WHOLE STORY OF HOW WE HAD BEEN MISTREATED AND WHY MY MOTHER HAD SENT ME TO TAKE REVENGE ON THOSE WHO HAD BEEN SO CRUEL TO US.
IF I DO NOT SUCCEED, SHE'LL CERTAINLY KILL HERSELF!
THIS ART THAT YOU REQUEST SHOULD HAVE SUFFICIENT CAUSE FOR ITS USE. AND I DO NOT BESTOW THESE TEACHINGS EASILY, BUT YOU ARE SINCERE.
I AM CONVINCED THAT YOU SPEAK THE TRUTH. FORMERLY I HAD A MOST DESTRUCTIVE PIECE OF MAGIC, CALLED 'DZA WITH THE PURPLE-BLACK FACE' TOGETHER WITH A DEATH-CAUSING MANTRA. IT IS VERY POWERFUL AND JUST RIGHT FOR YOUR PURPOSE.

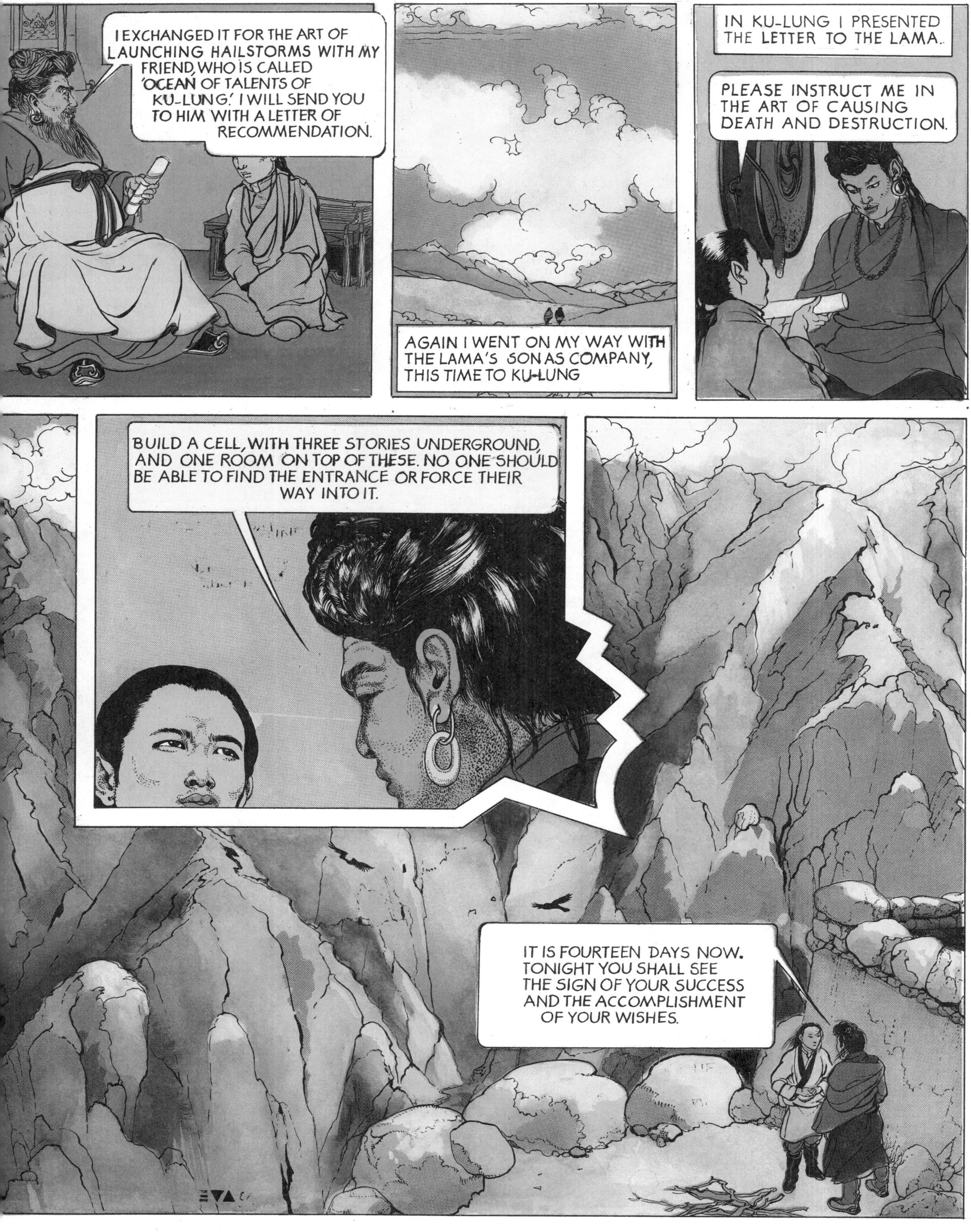
I EXCHANGED IT FOR THE ART OF LAUNCHING HAILSTORMS WITH MY FRIEND, WHO IS CALLED 'OCEAN OF TALENTS OF KU-LUNG.' I WILL SEND YOU TO HIM WITH A LETTER OF RECOMMENDATION.
AGAIN I WENT ON MY WAY WITH THE LAMA'S SON AS COMPANY, THIS TIME TO KU-LUNG
IN KU-LUNG I PRESENTED THE LETTER TO THE LAMA.
PLEASE INSTRUCT ME IN THE ART OF CAUSING DEATH AND DESTRUCTION.
BUILD A CELL, WITH THREE STORIES UNDERGROUND, AND ONE ROOM ON TOP OF THESE. NO ONE SHOULD BE ABLE TO FIND THE ENTRANCE OR FORCE THEIR WAY INTO IT.
IT IS FOURTEEN DAYS NOW. TONIGHT YOU SHALL SEE THE SIGN OF YOUR SUCCESS AND THE ACCOMPLISHMENT OF YOUR WISHES.

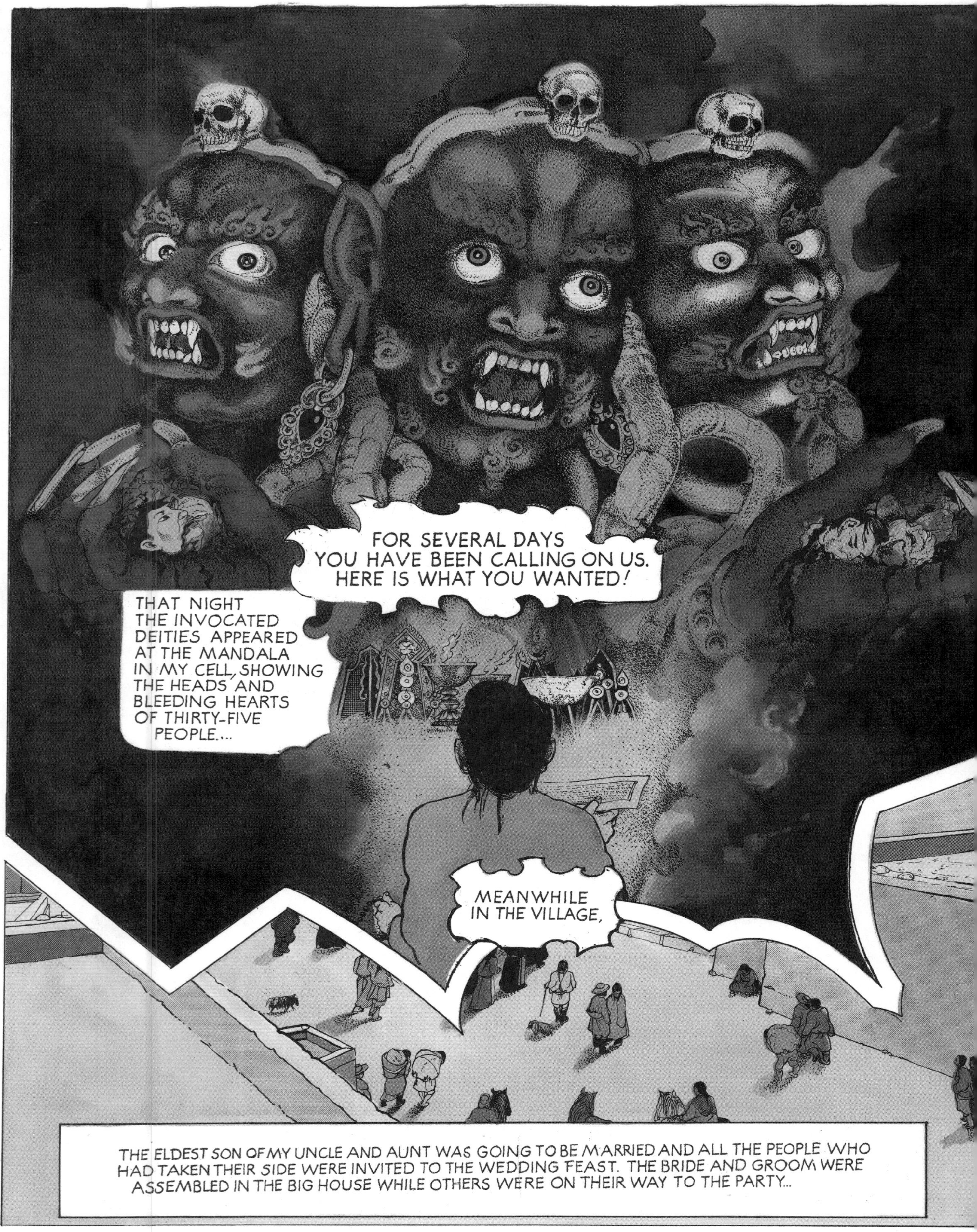
FOR SEVERAL DAYS YOU HAVE BEEN CALLING ON US. HERE IS WHAT YOU WANTED!
THAT NIGHT THE INVOCATED DEITIES APPEARED AT THE MANDALA IN MY CELL, SHOWING THE HEADS AND BLEEDING HEARTS OF THIRTY-FIVE PEOPLE....
MEANWHILE IN THE VILLAGE,
THE ELDEST SON OF MY UNCLE AND AUNT WAS GOING TO BE MARRIED AND ALL THE PEOPLE WHO HAD TAKEN THEIR SIDE WERE INVITED TO THE WEDDING FEAST. THE BRIDE AND GROOM WERE ASSEMBLED IN THE BIG HOUSE WHILE OTHERS WERE ON THEIR WAY TO THE PARTY...

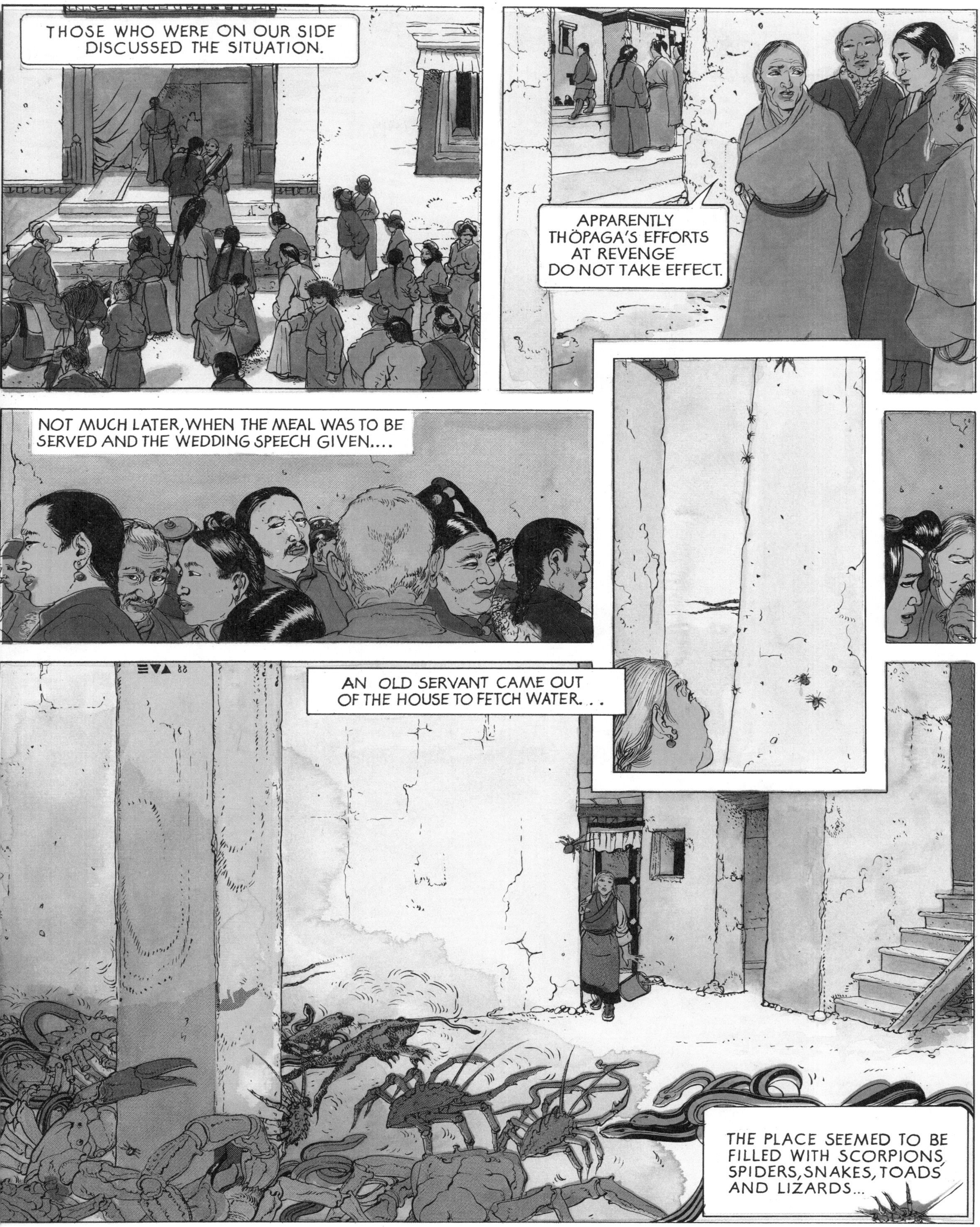

THOSE WHO WERE ON OUR SIDE DISCUSSED THE SITUATION.
APPARENTLY THÖPAGA'S EFFORTS AT REVENGE DO NOT TAKE EFFECT.
NOT MUCH LATER, WHEN THE MEAL WAS TO BE SERVED AND THE WEDDING SPEECH GIVEN....
AN OLD SERVANT CAME OUT OF THE HOUSE TO FETCH WATER...
THE PLACE SEEMED TO BE FILLED WITH SCORPIONS, SPIDERS, SNAKES, TOADS AND LIZARDS...

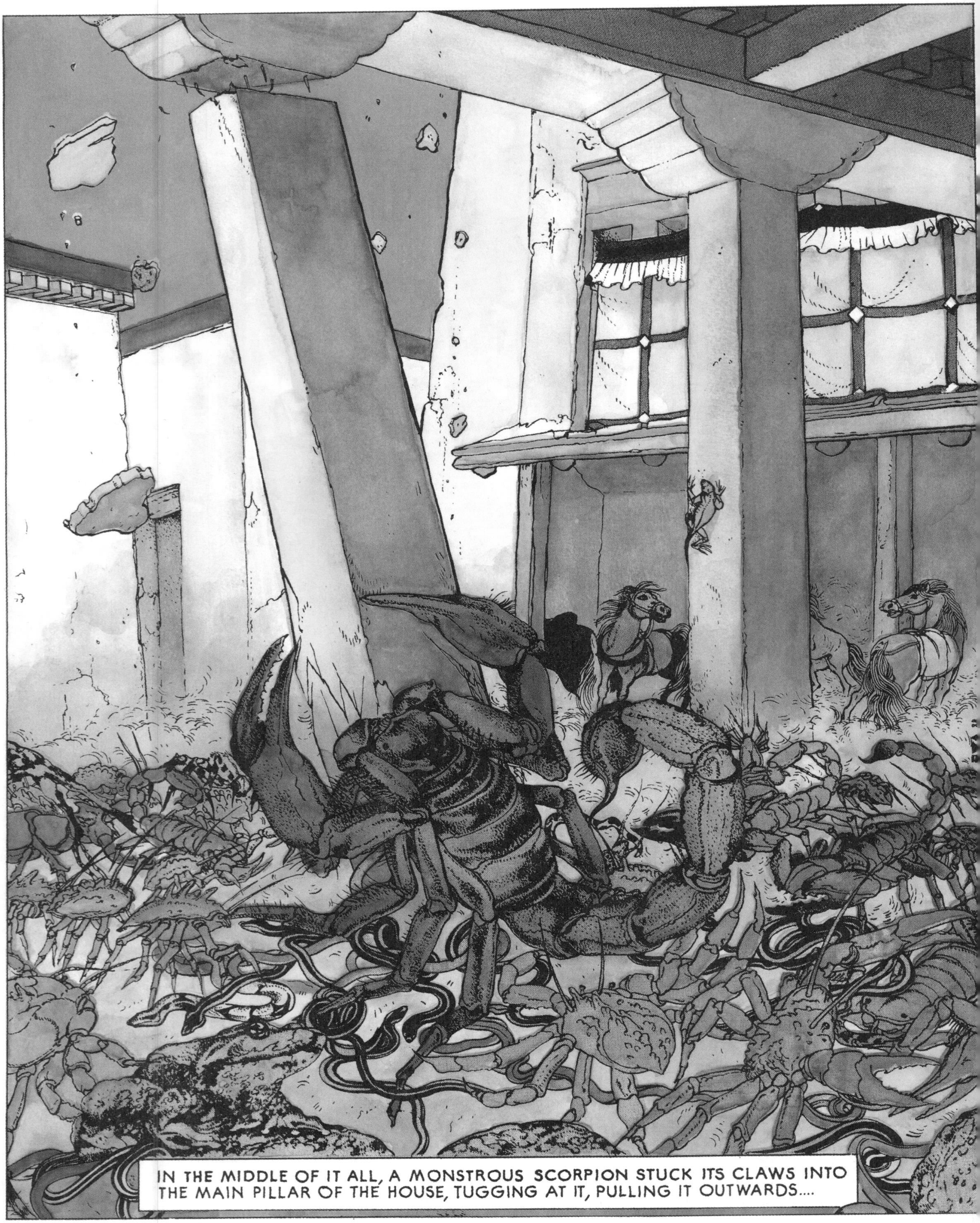
IN THE MIDDLE OF IT ALL, A MONSTROUS SCORPION STUCK ITS CLAWS INTO THE MAIN PILLAR OF THE HOUSE, TUGGING AT IT, PULLING IT OUTWARDS....

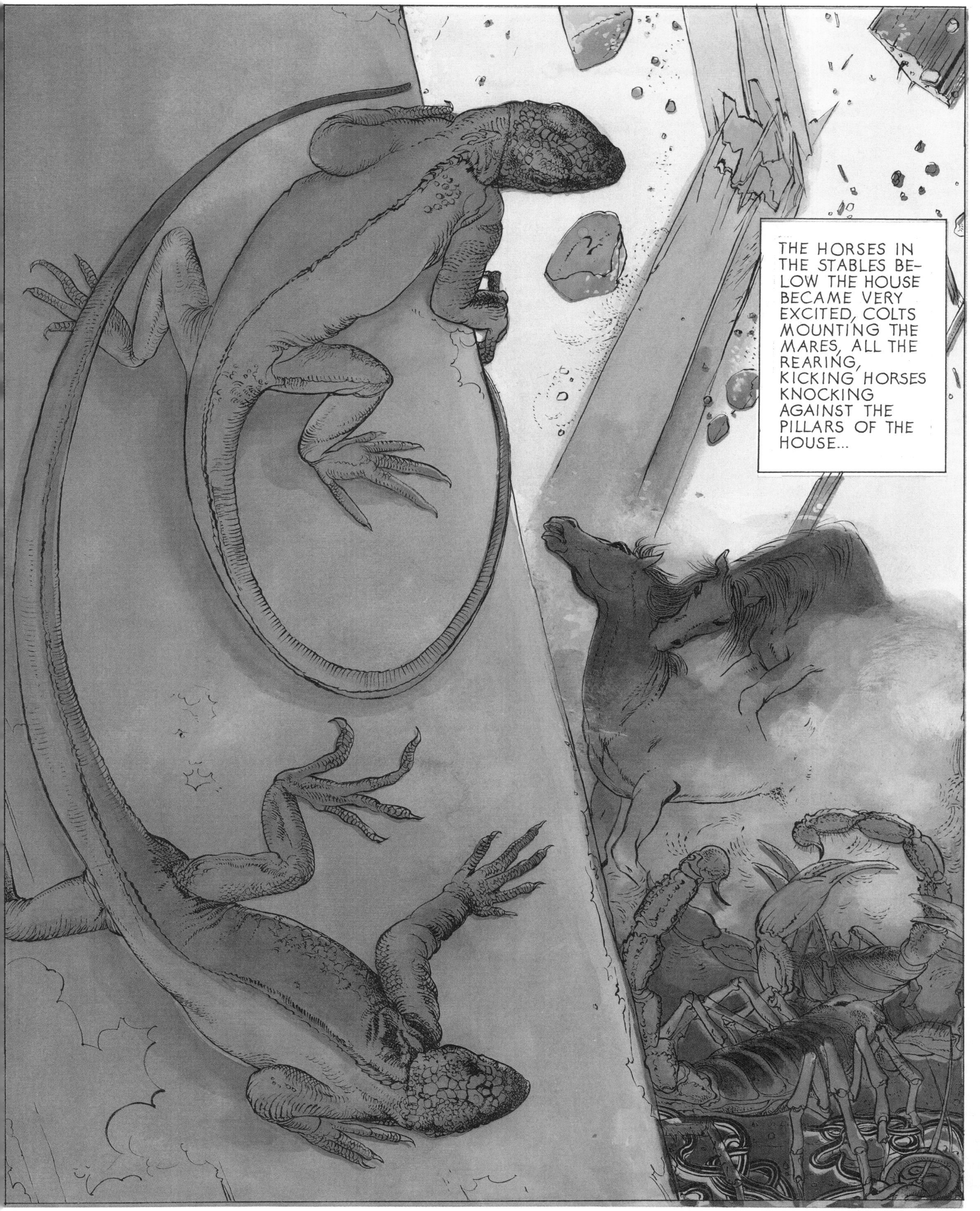
THE HORSES IN THE STABLES BE-LOW THE HOUSE BECAME VERY EXCITED, COLTS MOUNTING THE MARES, ALL THE REARING, KICKING HORSES KNOCKING AGAINST THE PILLARS OF THE HOUSE...

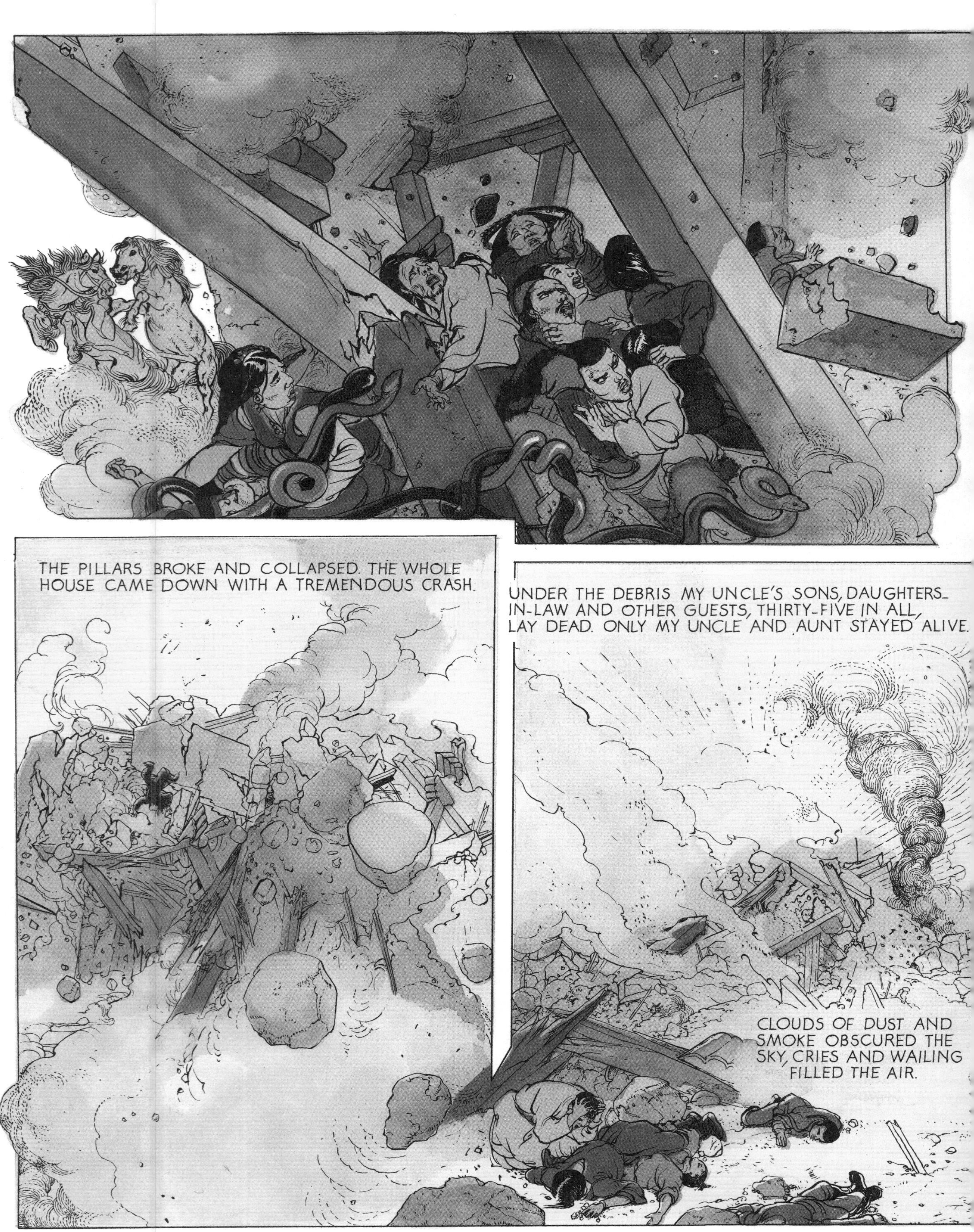
THE PILLARS BROKE AND COLLAPSED. THE WHOLE HOUSE CAME DOWN WITH A TREMENDOUS CRASH.
UNDER THE DEBRIS MY UNCLE'S SONS, DAUGHTERS-IN-LAW AND OTHER GUESTS, THIRTY-FIVE IN ALL, LAY DEAD. ONLY MY UNCLE AND AUNT STAYED ALIVE.
CLOUDS OF DUST AND SMOKE OBSCURED THE SKY, CRIES AND WAILING FILLED THE AIR.

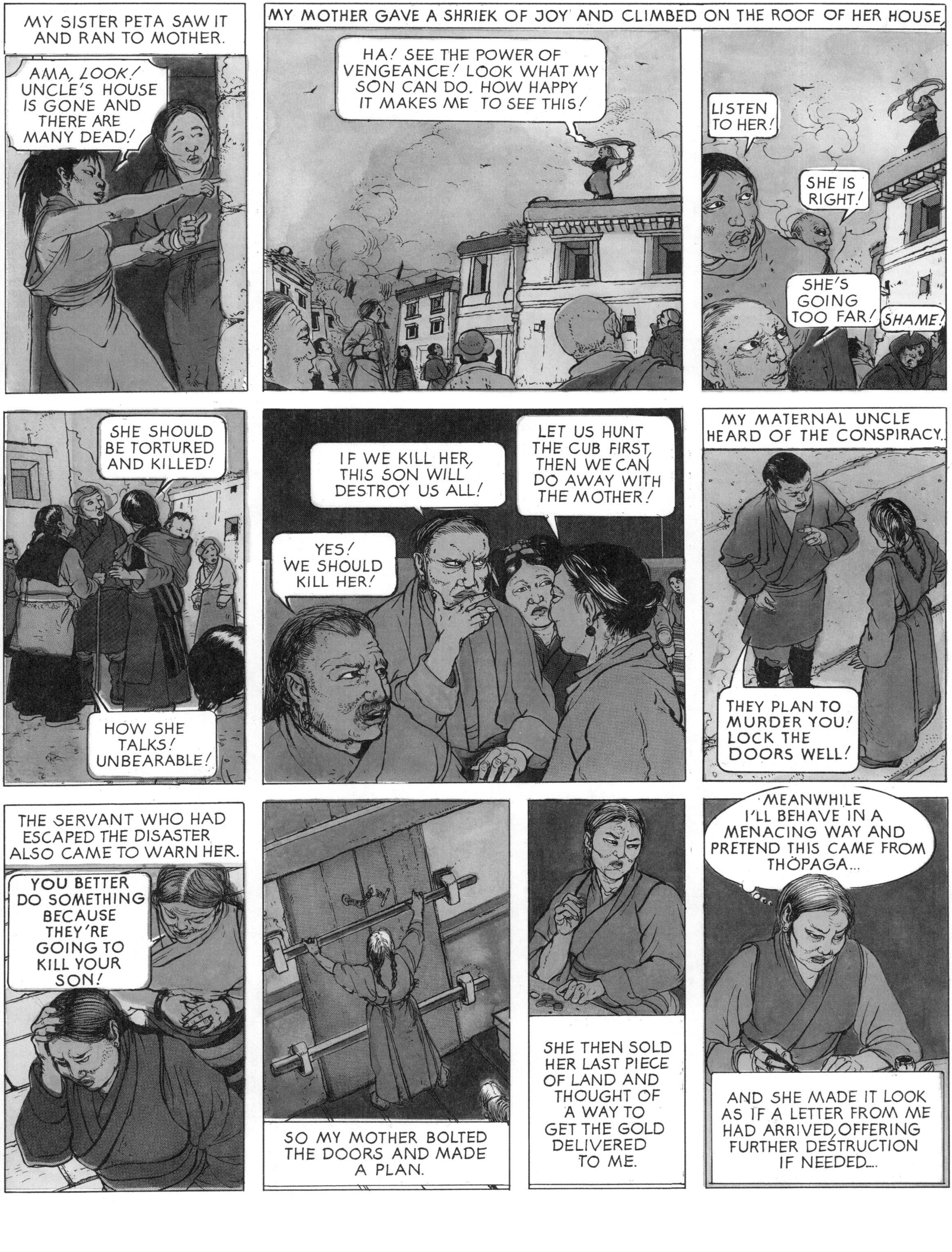
MY SISTER PETA SAW IT AND RAN TO MOTHER.
AMA, LOOK! UNCLE'S HOUSE IS GONE AND THERE ARE MANY DEAD!
MY MOTHER GAVE A SHRIEK OF JOY AND CLIMBED ON THE ROOF OF HER HOUSE,
HA! SEE THE POWER OF VENGEANCE! LOOK WHAT MY SON CAN DO. HOW HAPPY IT MAKES ME TO SEE THIS!
LISTEN TO HER!
SHE IS RIGHT!
SHE'S GOING TOO FAR!
SHAME!
SHE SHOULD BE TORTURED AND KILLED!
HOW SHE TALKS! UNBEARABLE!
IF WE KILL HER, THIS SON WILL DESTROY US ALL!
LET US HUNT THE CUB FIRST, THEN WE CAN DO AWAY WITH THE MOTHER!
YES! WE SHOULD KILL HER!
MY MATERNAL UNCLE HEARD OF THE CONSPIRACY..
THEY PLAN TO MURDER YOU! LOCK THE DOORS WELL!
THE SERVANT WHO HAD ESCAPED THE DISASTER ALSO CAME TO WARN HER.
YOU BETTER DO SOMETHING BECAUSE THEY'RE GOING TO KILL YOUR SON!
SO MY MOTHER BOLTED THE DOORS AND MADE A PLAN.
SHE THEN SOLD HER LAST PIECE OF LAND AND THOUGHT OF A WAY TO GET THE GOLD DELIVERED TO ME.
MEANWHILE I'LL BEHAVE IN A MENACING WAY AND PRETEND THIS CAME FROM THÖPAGA...
AND SHE MADE IT LOOK AS IF A LETTER FROM ME HAD ARRIVED, OFFERING FURTHER DESTRUCTION IF NEEDED....

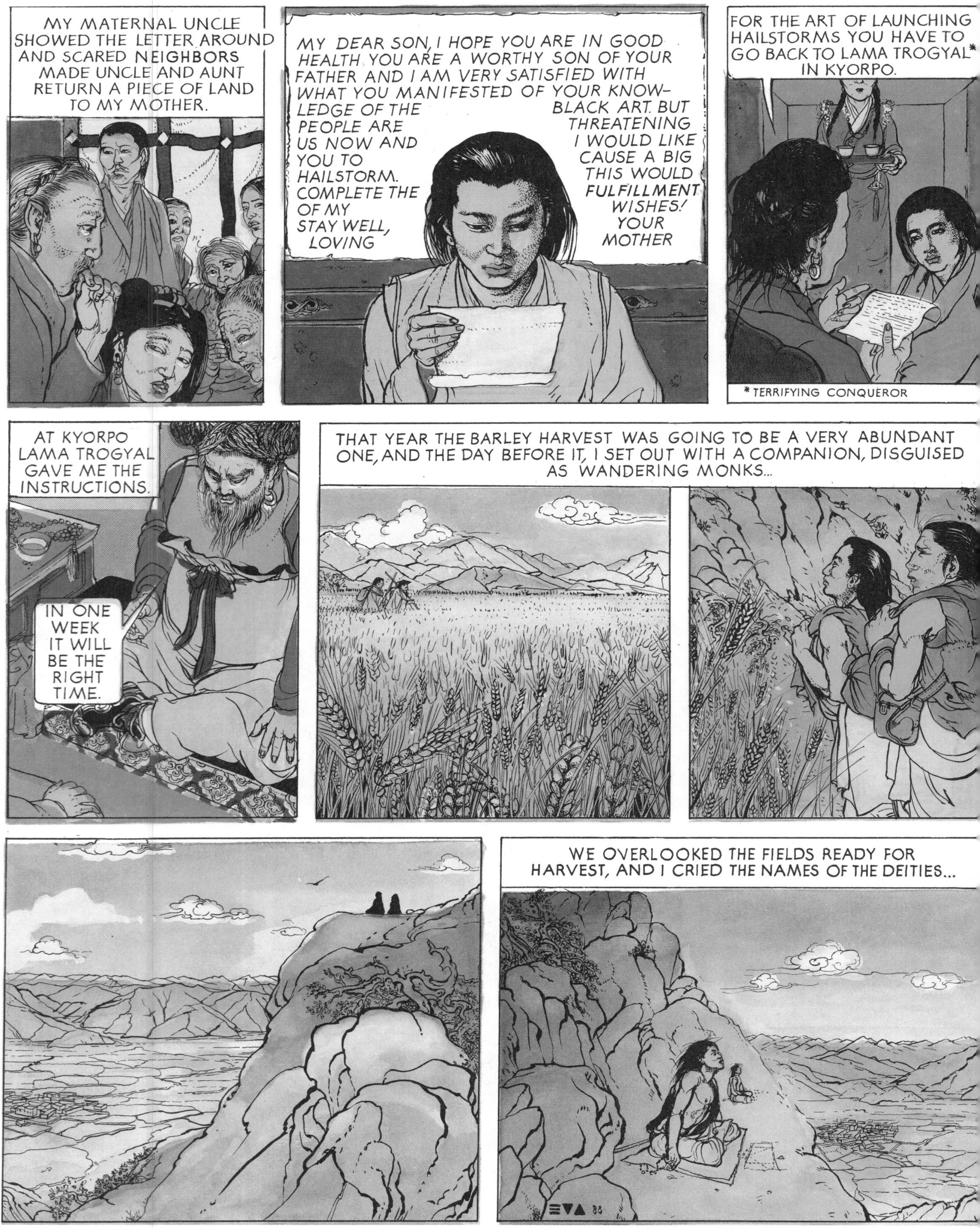
MY MATERNAL UNCLE SHOWED THE LETTER AROUND AND SCARED NEIGHBORS MADE UNCLE AND AUNT RETURN A PIECE OF LAND TO MY MOTHER.
MY DEAR SON, I HOPE YOU ARE IN GOOD HEALTH. YOU ARE A WORTHY SON OF YOUR FATHER AND I AM VERY SATISFIED WITH WHAT YOU MANIFESTED OF YOUR KNOW-
LEDGE OF THE BLACK ART. BUT
PEOPLE ARE THREATENING
US NOW AND I WOULD LIKE
YOU TO CAUSE A BIG
HAILSTORM. THIS WOULD
COMPLETE THE FULFILLMENT
OF MY WISHES!
STAY WELL, YOUR
LOVING MOTHER
FOR THE ART OF LAUNCHING HAILSTORMS YOU HAVE TO GO BACK TO LAMA TROGYAL* IN KYORPO.
*TERRIFYING CONQUEROR
AT KYORPO LAMA TROGYAL GAVE ME THE INSTRUCTIONS.
IN ONE WEEK IT WILL BE THE RIGHT TIME.
THAT YEAR THE BARLEY HARVEST WAS GOING TO BE A VERY ABUNDANT ONE, AND THE DAY BEFORE IT, I SET OUT WITH A COMPANION, DISGUISED AS WANDERING MONKS...
WE OVERLOOKED THE FIELDS READY FOR HARVEST, AND I CRIED THE NAMES OF THE DEITIES...
EVA 88

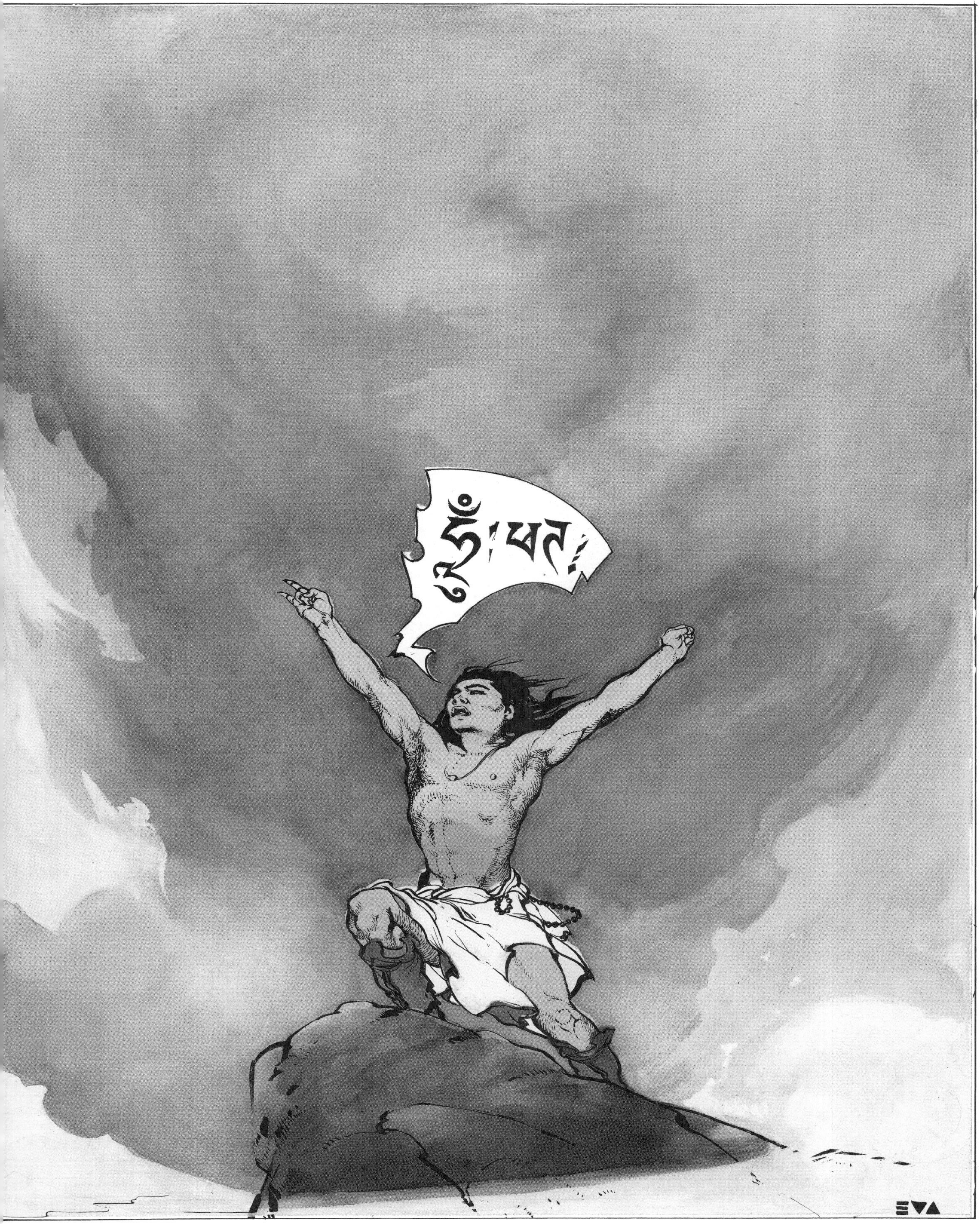
ཧཱུྃ་ཕཊ།
EVA

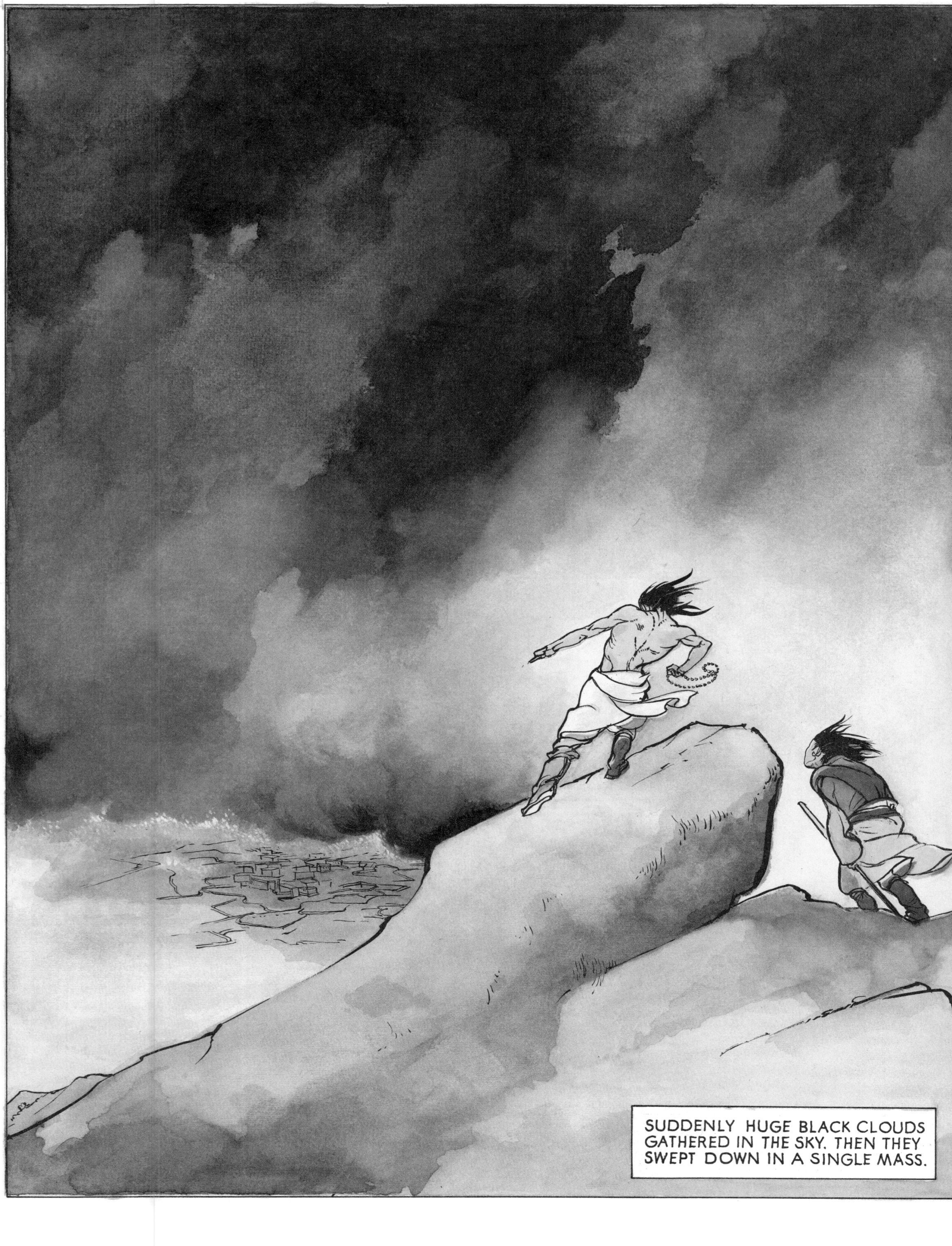
SUDDENLY HUGE BLACK CLOUDS GATHERED IN THE SKY. THEN THEY SWEPT DOWN IN A SINGLE MASS.

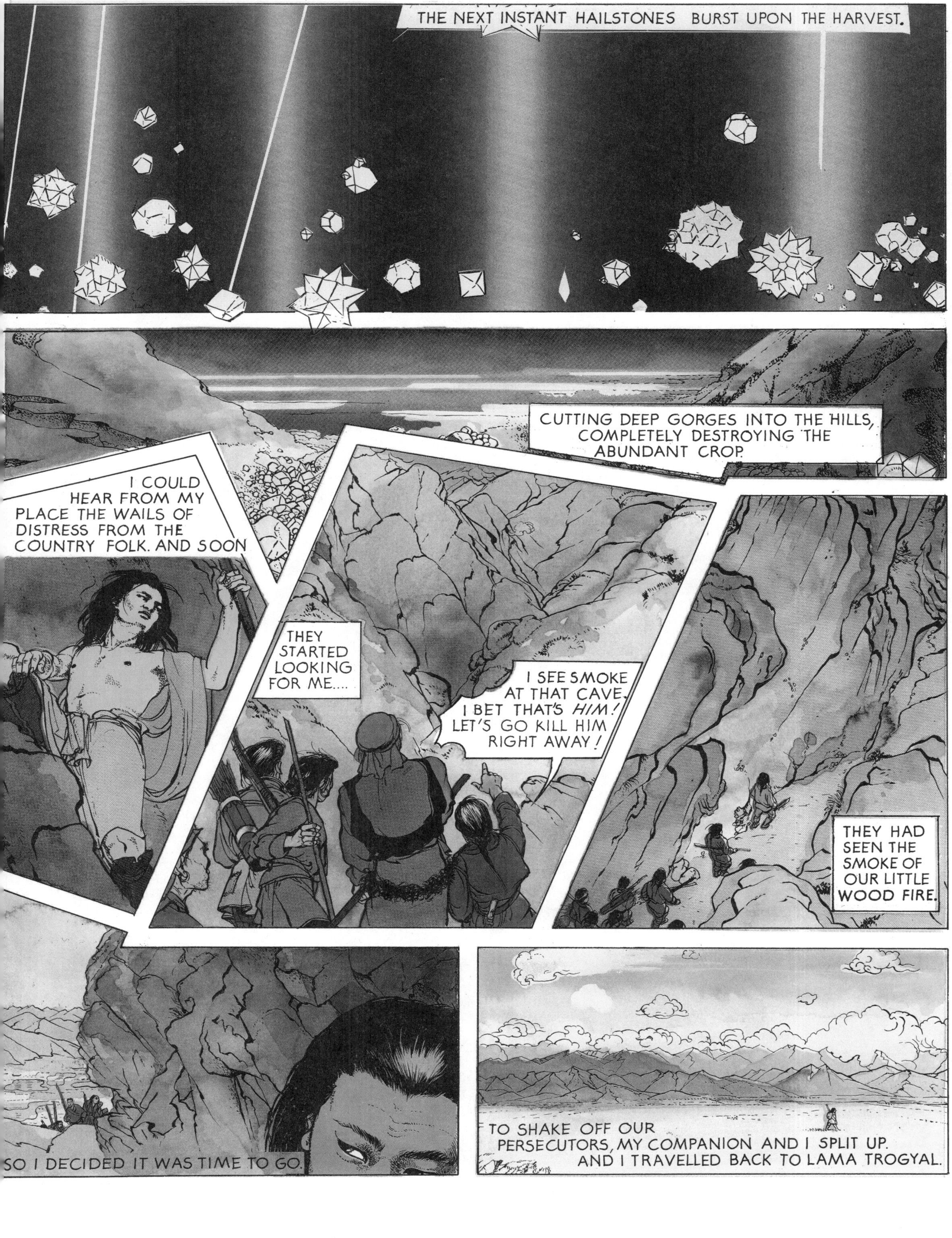
THE NEXT INSTANT HAILSTONES BURST UPON THE HARVEST.
CUTTING DEEP GORGES INTO THE HILLS, COMPLETELY DESTROYING THE ABUNDANT CROP.
I COULD HEAR FROM MY PLACE THE WAILS OF DISTRESS FROM THE COUNTRY FOLK. AND SOON
THEY STARTED LOOKING FOR ME....
I SEE SMOKE AT THAT CAVE. I BET THAT'S *HIM*! LET'S GO KILL HIM RIGHT AWAY!
THEY HAD SEEN THE SMOKE OF OUR LITTLE WOOD FIRE.
SO I DECIDED IT WAS TIME TO GO.
TO SHAKE OFF OUR PERSECUTORS, MY COMPANION AND I SPLIT UP. AND I TRAVELLED BACK TO LAMA TROGYAL.

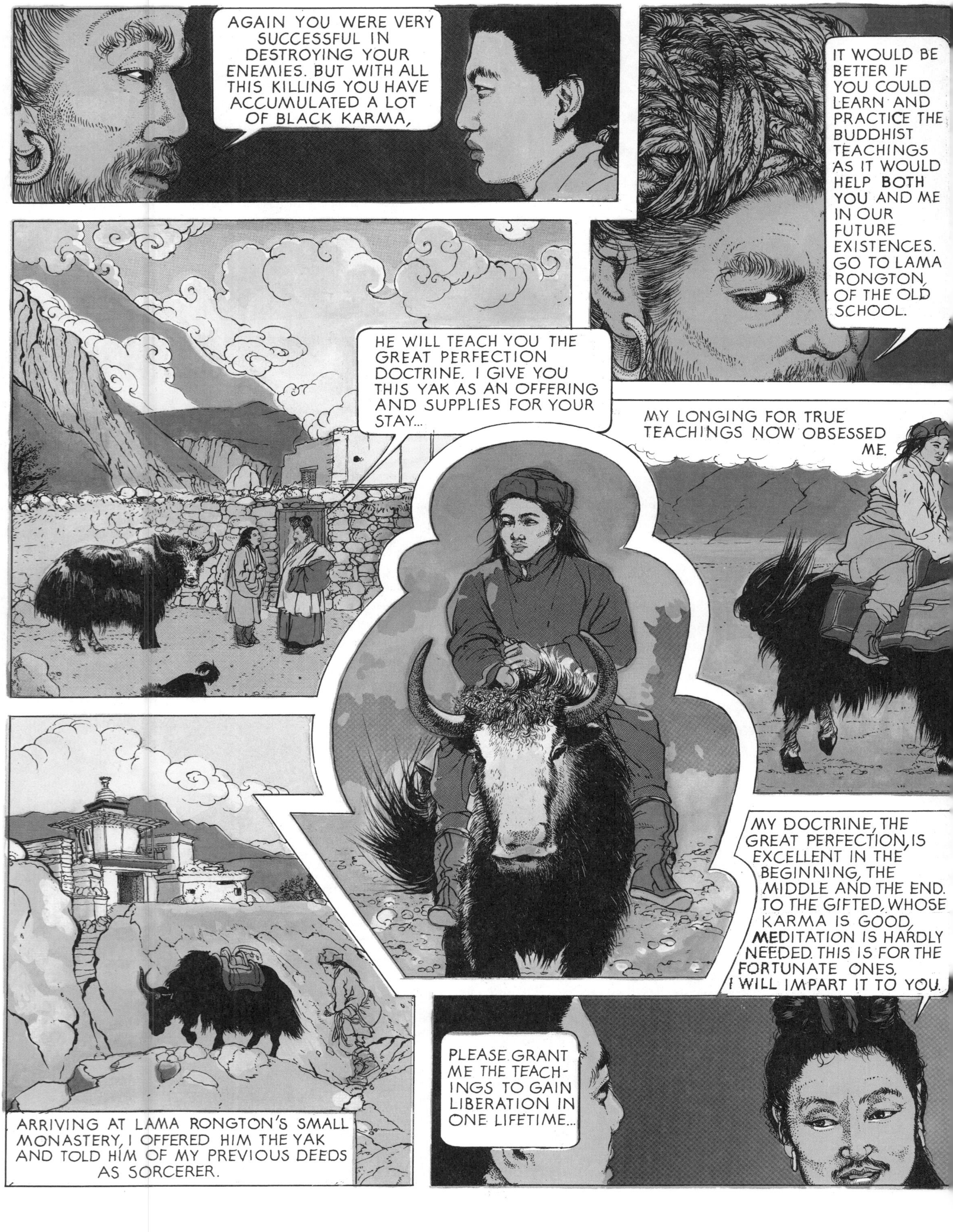
AGAIN YOU WERE VERY SUCCESSFUL IN DESTROYING YOUR ENEMIES. BUT WITH ALL THIS KILLING YOU HAVE ACCUMULATED A LOT OF BLACK KARMA,
IT WOULD BE BETTER IF YOU COULD LEARN AND PRACTICE THE BUDDHIST TEACHINGS AS IT WOULD HELP BOTH YOU AND ME IN OUR FUTURE EXISTENCES. GO TO LAMA RONGTON, OF THE OLD SCHOOL.
HE WILL TEACH YOU THE GREAT PERFECTION DOCTRINE. I GIVE YOU THIS YAK AS AN OFFERING AND SUPPLIES FOR YOUR STAY...
MY LONGING FOR TRUE TEACHINGS NOW OBSESSED ME.
ARRIVING AT LAMA RONGTON'S SMALL MONASTERY, I OFFERED HIM THE YAK AND TOLD HIM OF MY PREVIOUS DEEDS AS SORCERER.
PLEASE GRANT ME THE TEACHINGS TO GAIN LIBERATION IN ONE LIFETIME...
MY DOCTRINE, THE GREAT PERFECTION, IS EXCELLENT IN THE BEGINNING, THE MIDDLE AND THE END. TO THE GIFTED, WHOSE KARMA IS GOOD, MEDITATION IS HARDLY NEEDED. THIS IS FOR THE FORTUNATE ONES, I WILL IMPART IT TO YOU.

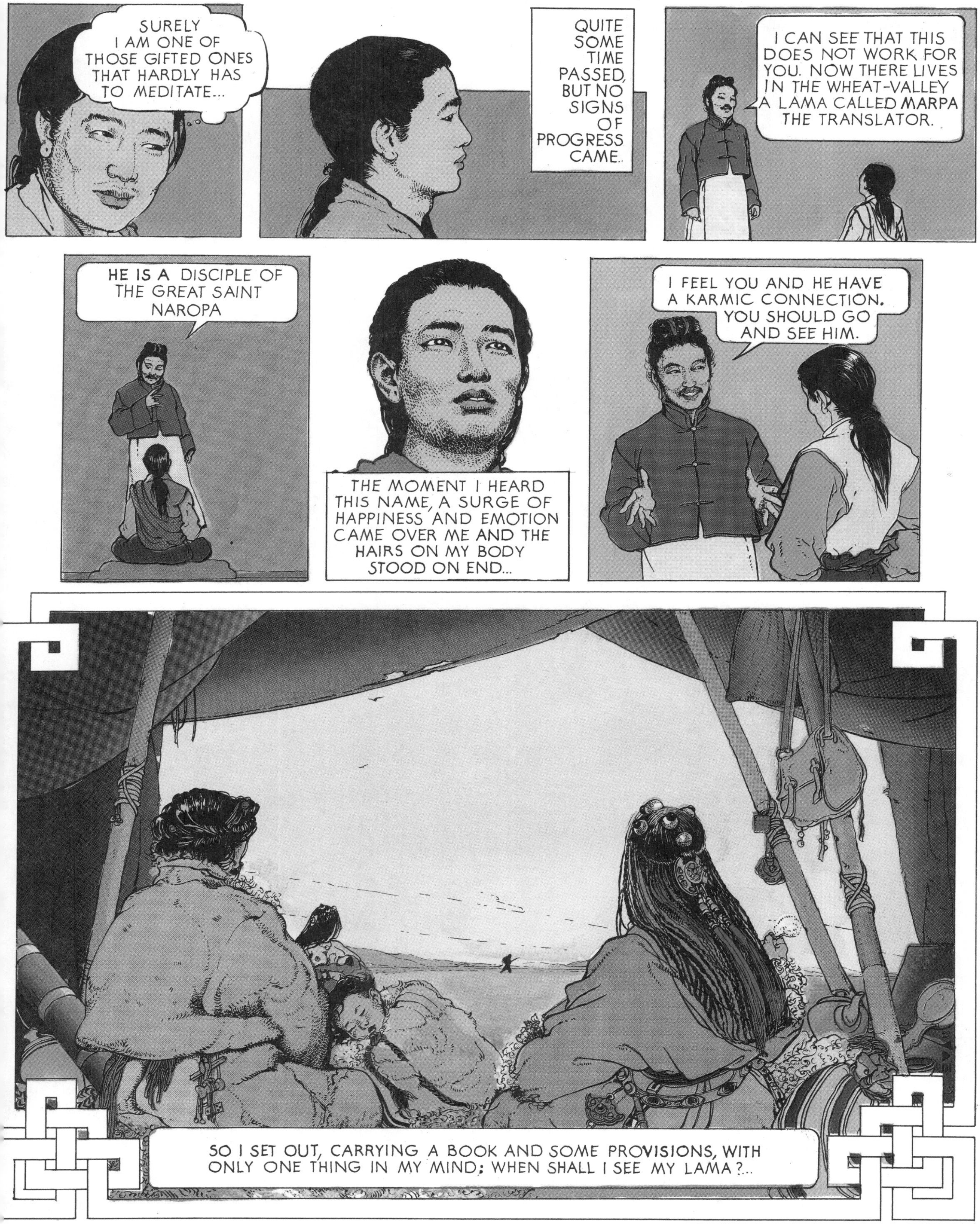
SURELY I AM ONE OF THOSE GIFTED ONES THAT HARDLY HAS TO MEDITATE...
QUITE SOME TIME PASSED, BUT NO SIGNS OF PROGRESS CAME..
I CAN SEE THAT THIS DOES NOT WORK FOR YOU. NOW THERE LIVES IN THE WHEAT-VALLEY A LAMA CALLED MARPA THE TRANSLATOR.
HE IS A DISCIPLE OF THE GREAT SAINT NAROPA
THE MOMENT I HEARD THIS NAME, A SURGE OF HAPPINESS AND EMOTION CAME OVER ME AND THE HAIRS ON MY BODY STOOD ON END...
I FEEL YOU AND HE HAVE A KARMIC CONNECTION. YOU SHOULD GO AND SEE HIM.
SO I SET OUT, CARRYING A BOOK AND SOME PROVISIONS, WITH ONLY ONE THING IN MY MIND: WHEN SHALL I SEE MY LAMA?...

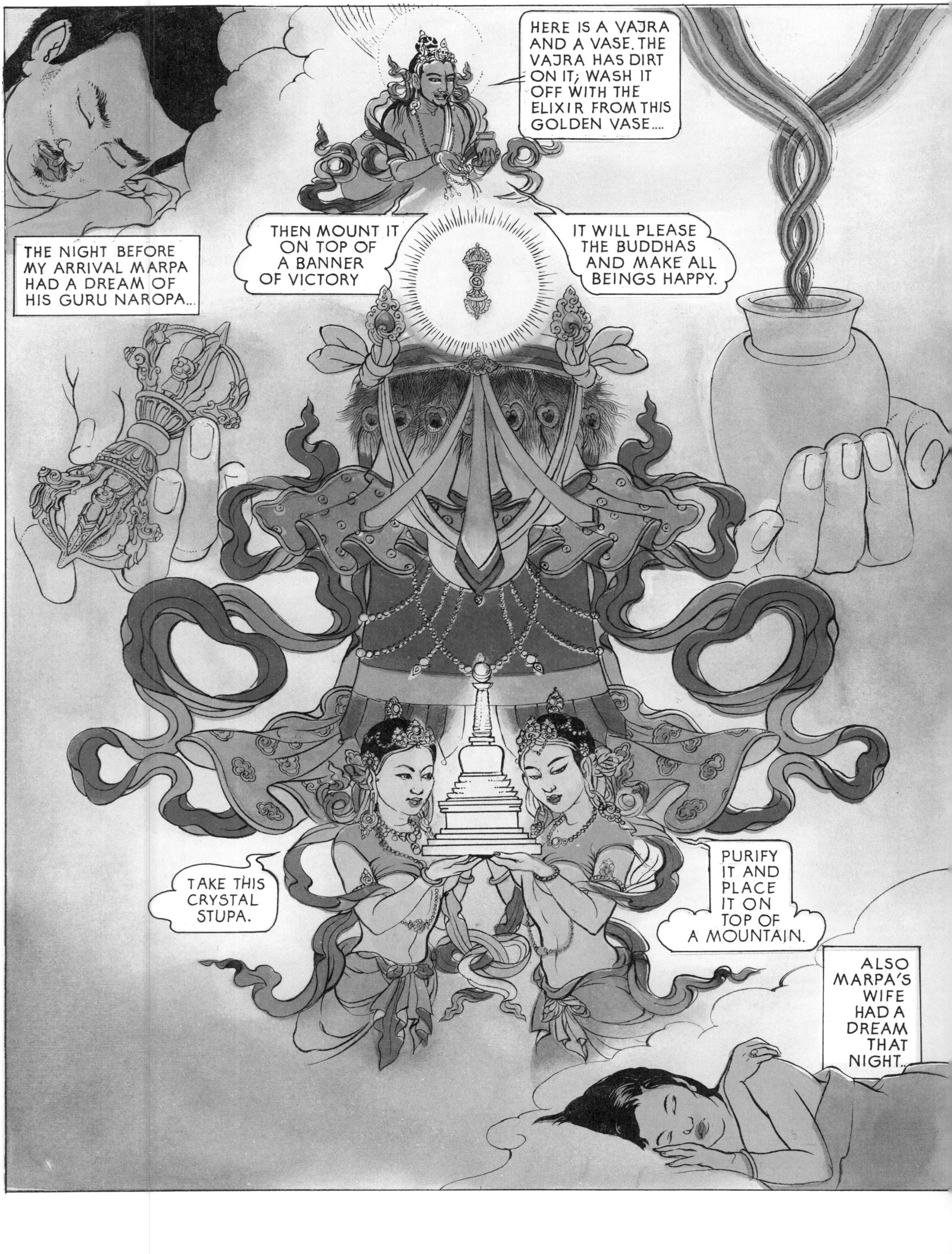
THE NIGHT BEFORE MY ARRIVAL MARPA HAD A DREAM OF HIS GURU NAROPA...
HERE IS A VAJRA AND A VASE. THE VAJRA HAS DIRT ON IT; WASH IT OFF WITH THE ELIXIR FROM THIS GOLDEN VASE....
THEN MOUNT IT ON TOP OF A BANNER OF VICTORY
IT WILL PLEASE THE BUDDHAS AND MAKE ALL BEINGS HAPPY.
TAKE THIS CRYSTAL STUPA.
PURIFY IT AND PLACE IT ON TOP OF A MOUNTAIN.
ALSO MARPA'S WIFE HAD A DREAM THAT NIGHT..

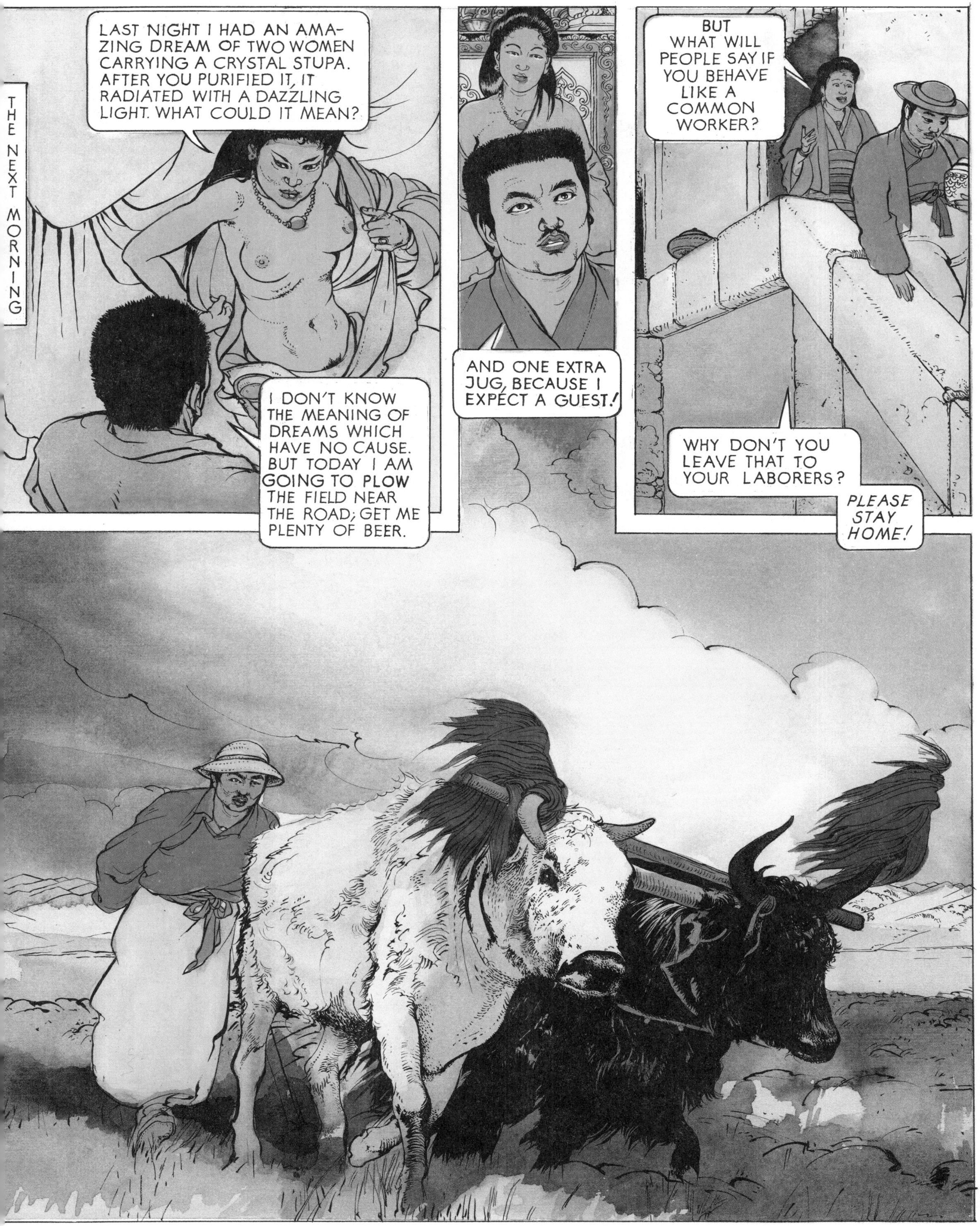
THE NEXT MORNING
LAST NIGHT I HAD AN AMAZING DREAM OF TWO WOMEN CARRYING A CRYSTAL STUPA. AFTER YOU PURIFIED IT, IT RADIATED WITH A DAZZLING LIGHT. WHAT COULD IT MEAN?
I DON'T KNOW THE MEANING OF DREAMS WHICH HAVE NO CAUSE. BUT TODAY I AM GOING TO PLOW THE FIELD NEAR THE ROAD; GET ME PLENTY OF BEER.
AND ONE EXTRA JUG, BECAUSE I EXPECT A GUEST!
BUT WHAT WILL PEOPLE SAY IF YOU BEHAVE LIKE A COMMON WORKER?
WHY DON'T YOU LEAVE THAT TO YOUR LABORERS?
PLEASE STAY HOME!

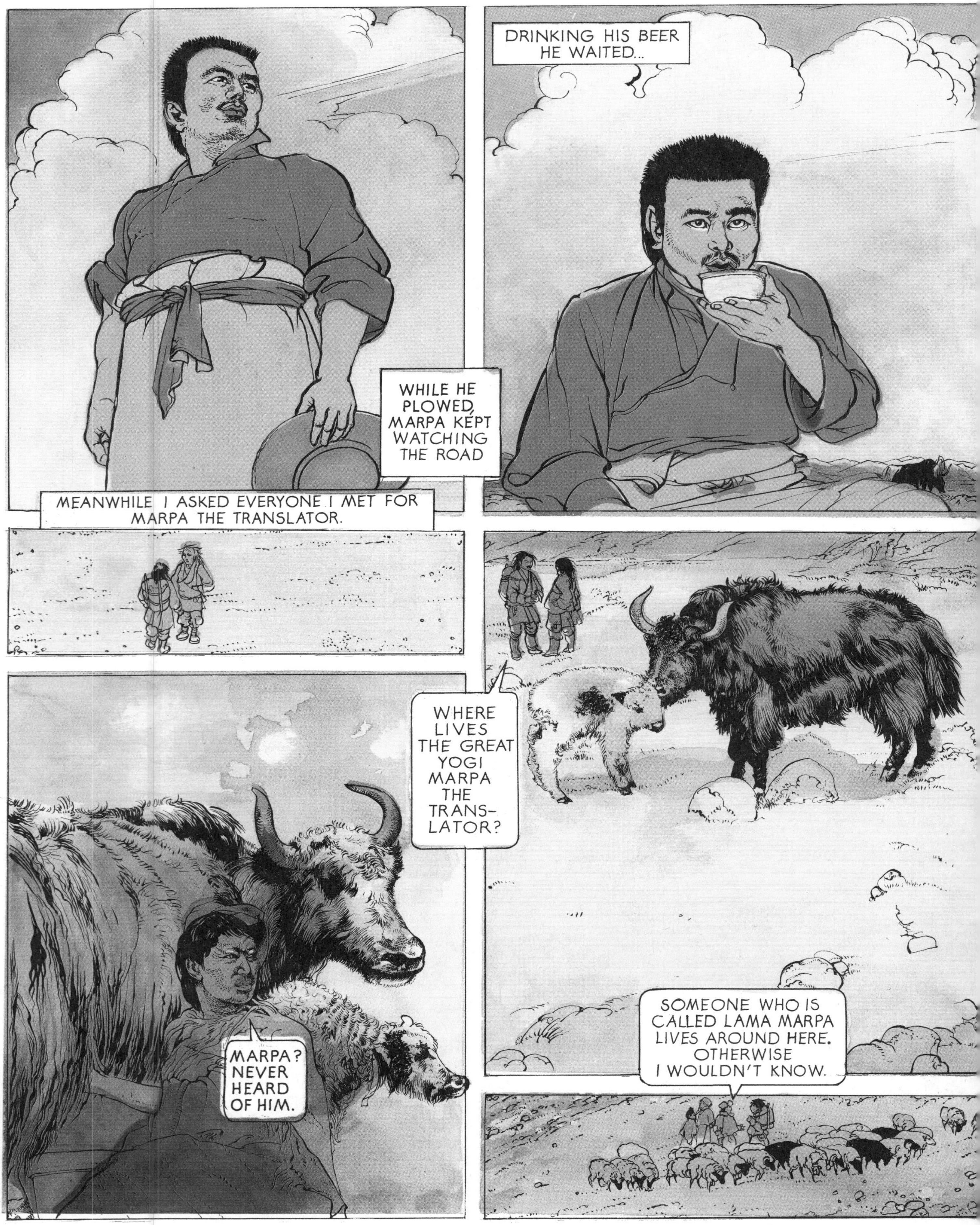
WHILE HE PLOWED, MARPA KEPT WATCHING THE ROAD
DRINKING HIS BEER HE WAITED...
MEANWHILE I ASKED EVERYONE I MET FOR MARPA THE TRANSLATOR.
WHERE LIVES THE GREAT YOGI MARPA THE TRANS-LATOR?
MARPA? NEVER HEARD OF HIM.
SOMEONE WHO IS CALLED LAMA MARPA LIVES AROUND HERE. OTHERWISE I WOULDN'T KNOW.

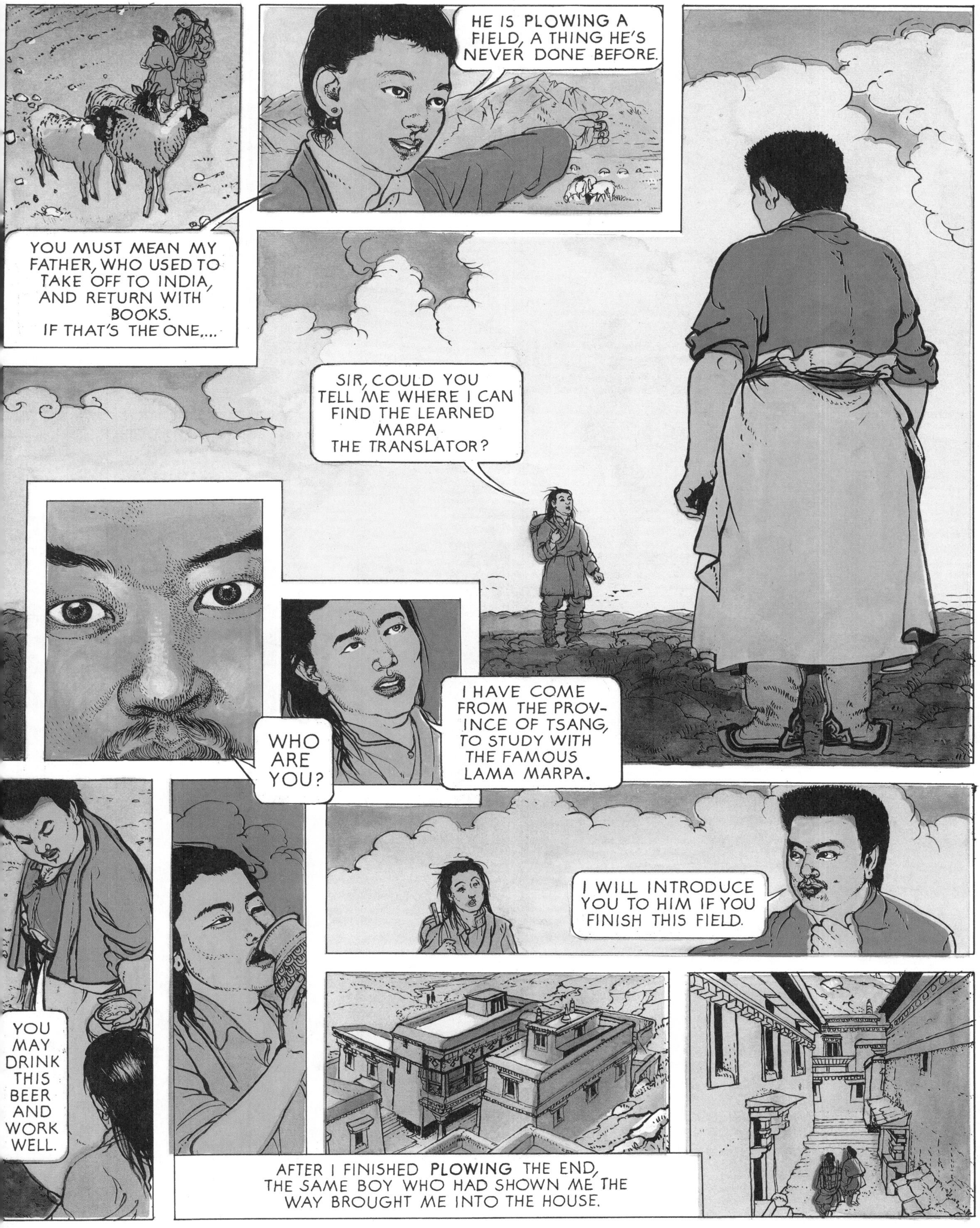
HE IS PLOWING A FIELD, A THING HE'S NEVER DONE BEFORE.
YOU MUST MEAN MY FATHER, WHO USED TO TAKE OFF TO INDIA, AND RETURN WITH BOOKS. IF THAT'S THE ONE,...
SIR, COULD YOU TELL ME WHERE I CAN FIND THE LEARNED MARPA THE TRANSLATOR?
WHO ARE YOU?
I HAVE COME FROM THE PROVINCE OF TSANG, TO STUDY WITH THE FAMOUS LAMA MARPA.
I WILL INTRODUCE YOU TO HIM IF YOU FINISH THIS FIELD.
YOU MAY DRINK THIS BEER AND WORK WELL.
AFTER I FINISHED PLOWING THE END, THE SAME BOY WHO HAD SHOWN ME THE WAY BROUGHT ME INTO THE HOUSE.

I AM MARPA HIMSELF. YOU MAY PROSTRATE NOW!

I RELATED MY HISTORY, OFFERED BODY, SPEECH AND MIND, AND ASKED TO BE TAKEN CARE OF.

IF YOU WANT SPIRITUAL INSTRUCTION FROM ME, YOU WILL HAVE TO FIND YOUR FOOD AND CLOTHING YOURSELF.

IT IS QUITE TRUE THAT YOU ARE AN ADEPT IN SORCERY. I'LL CALL YOU GREAT SORCERER. YOU SHOULD HAVE PATIENCE.

AND SINCE YOU SEEM TO HAVE PLENTY OF ENERGY...

I WOULD LIKE YOU TO BUILD A HOUSE FOR MY SON. WHEN YOU HAVE COMPLETED IT, I SHALL TEACH YOU AND SUPPLY YOU WITH FOOD AND WHATEVER YOU NEED DURING YOUR STUDY.

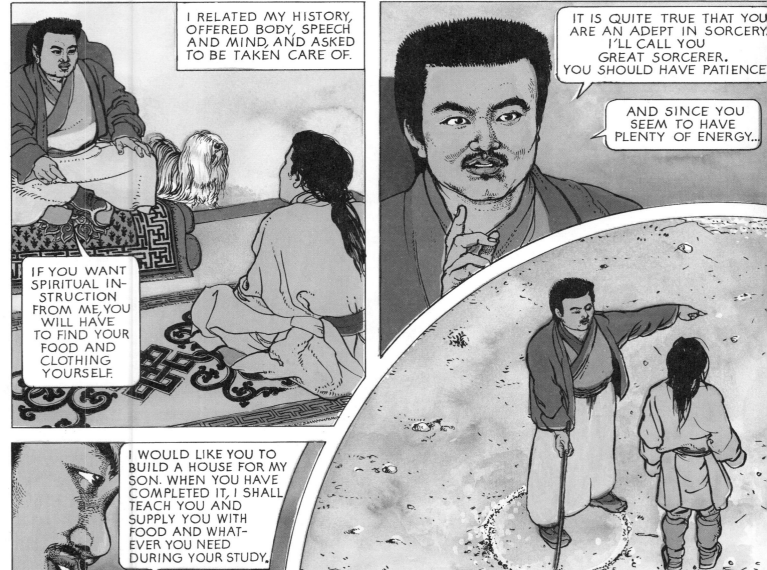

HE THEN TOOK ME TO THE EAST OF A MOUNTAIN RIDGE AND DESCRIBED A CIRCULAR STRUCTURE, ORDERING ME TO BEGIN BUILDING THERE.

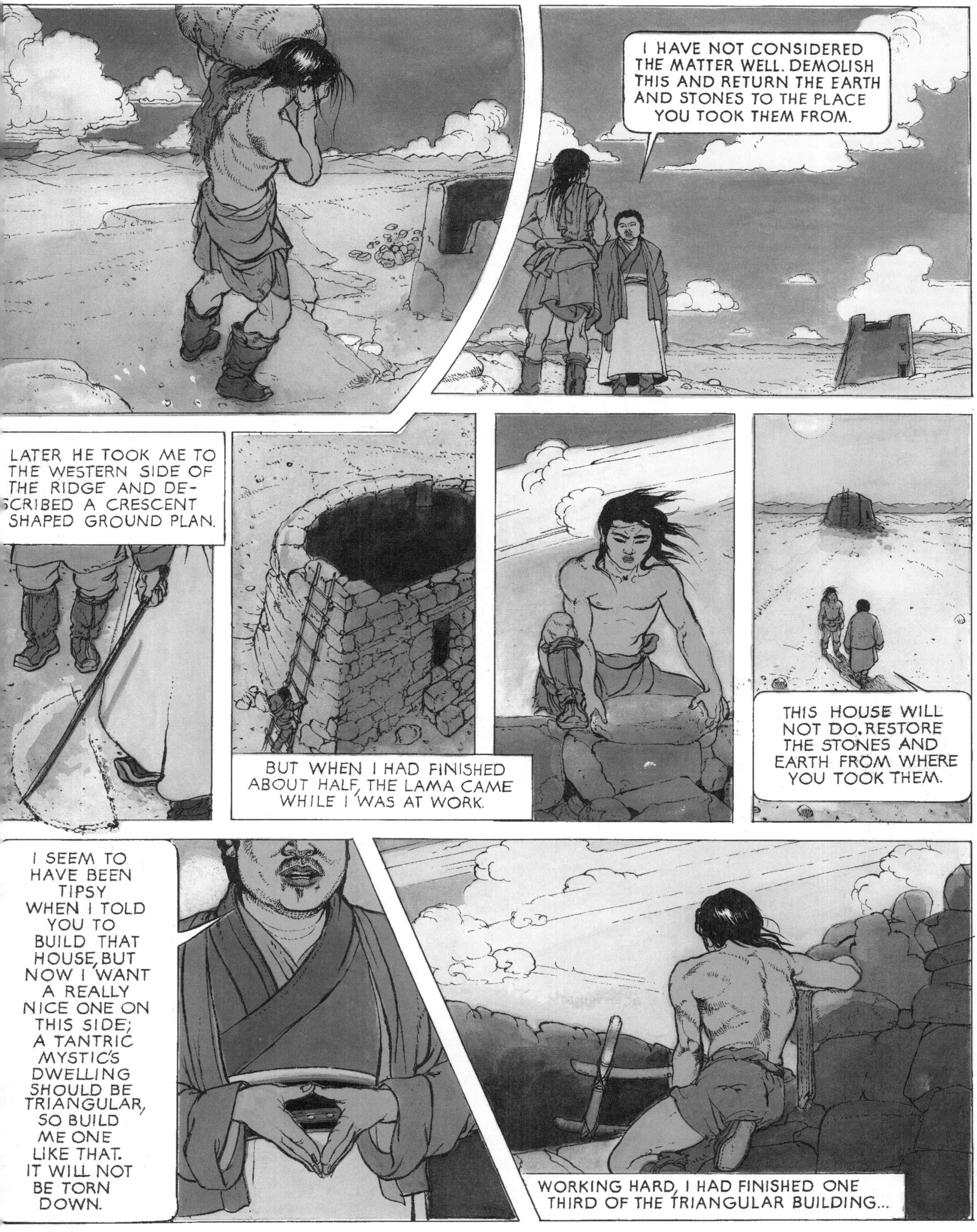
I HAVE NOT CONSIDERED THE MATTER WELL. DEMOLISH THIS AND RETURN THE EARTH AND STONES TO THE PLACE YOU TOOK THEM FROM.
LATER HE TOOK ME TO THE WESTERN SIDE OF THE RIDGE AND DESCRIBED A CRESCENT SHAPED GROUND PLAN.
BUT WHEN I HAD FINISHED ABOUT HALF, THE LAMA CAME WHILE I WAS AT WORK.
THIS HOUSE WILL NOT DO. RESTORE THE STONES AND EARTH FROM WHERE YOU TOOK THEM.
I SEEM TO HAVE BEEN TIPSY WHEN I TOLD YOU TO BUILD THAT HOUSE, BUT NOW I WANT A REALLY NICE ONE ON THIS SIDE; A TANTRIC MYSTIC'S DWELLING SHOULD BE TRIANGULAR, SO BUILD ME ONE LIKE THAT. IT WILL NOT BE TORN DOWN.
WORKING HARD, I HAD FINISHED ONE THIRD OF THE TRIANGULAR BUILDING...

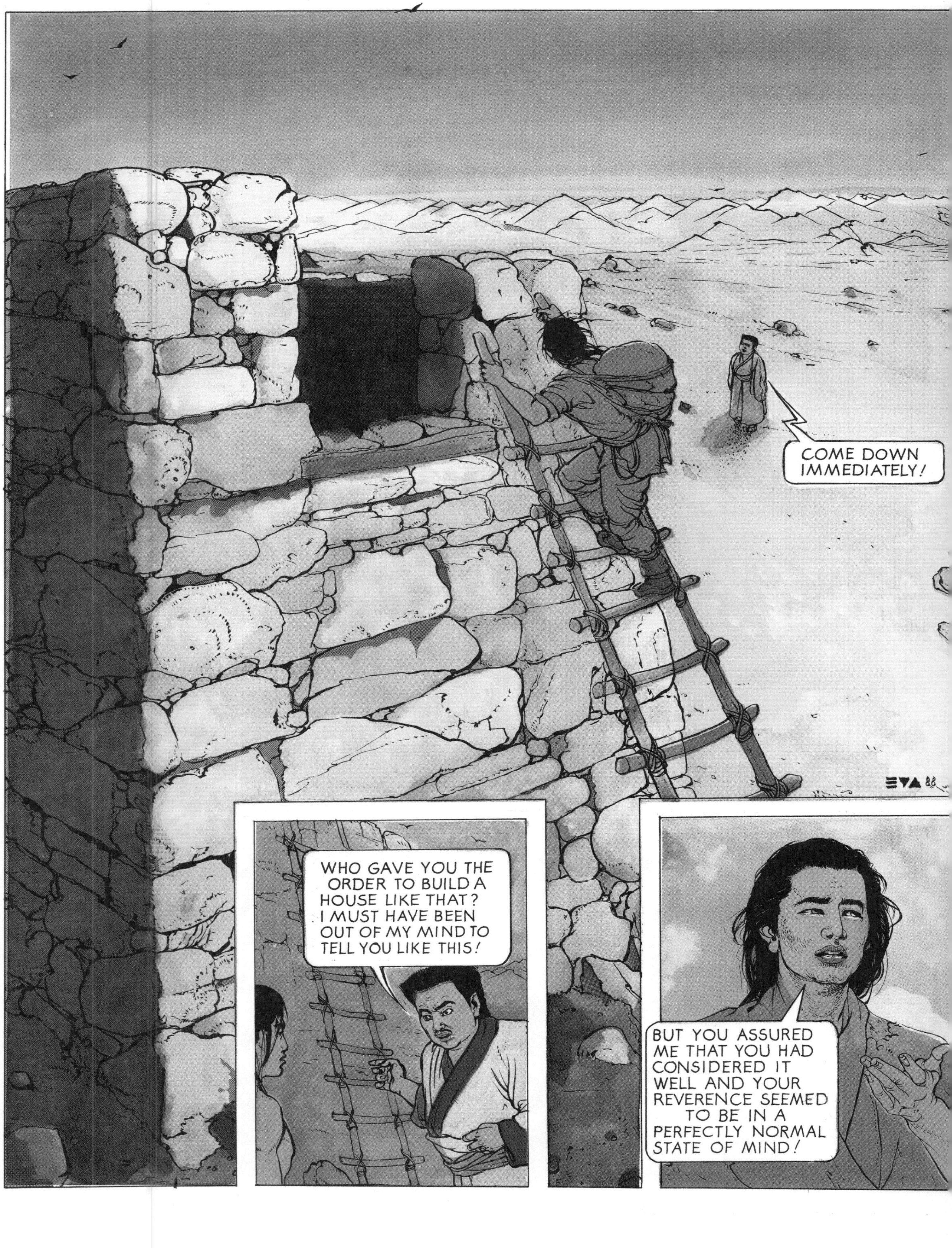
COME DOWN IMMEDIATELY!
EVA 88
WHO GAVE YOU THE ORDER TO BUILD A HOUSE LIKE THAT? I MUST HAVE BEEN OUT OF MY MIND TO TELL YOU LIKE THIS!
BUT YOU ASSURED ME THAT YOU HAD CONSIDERED IT WELL AND YOUR REVERENCE SEEMED TO BE IN A PERFECTLY NORMAL STATE OF MIND!

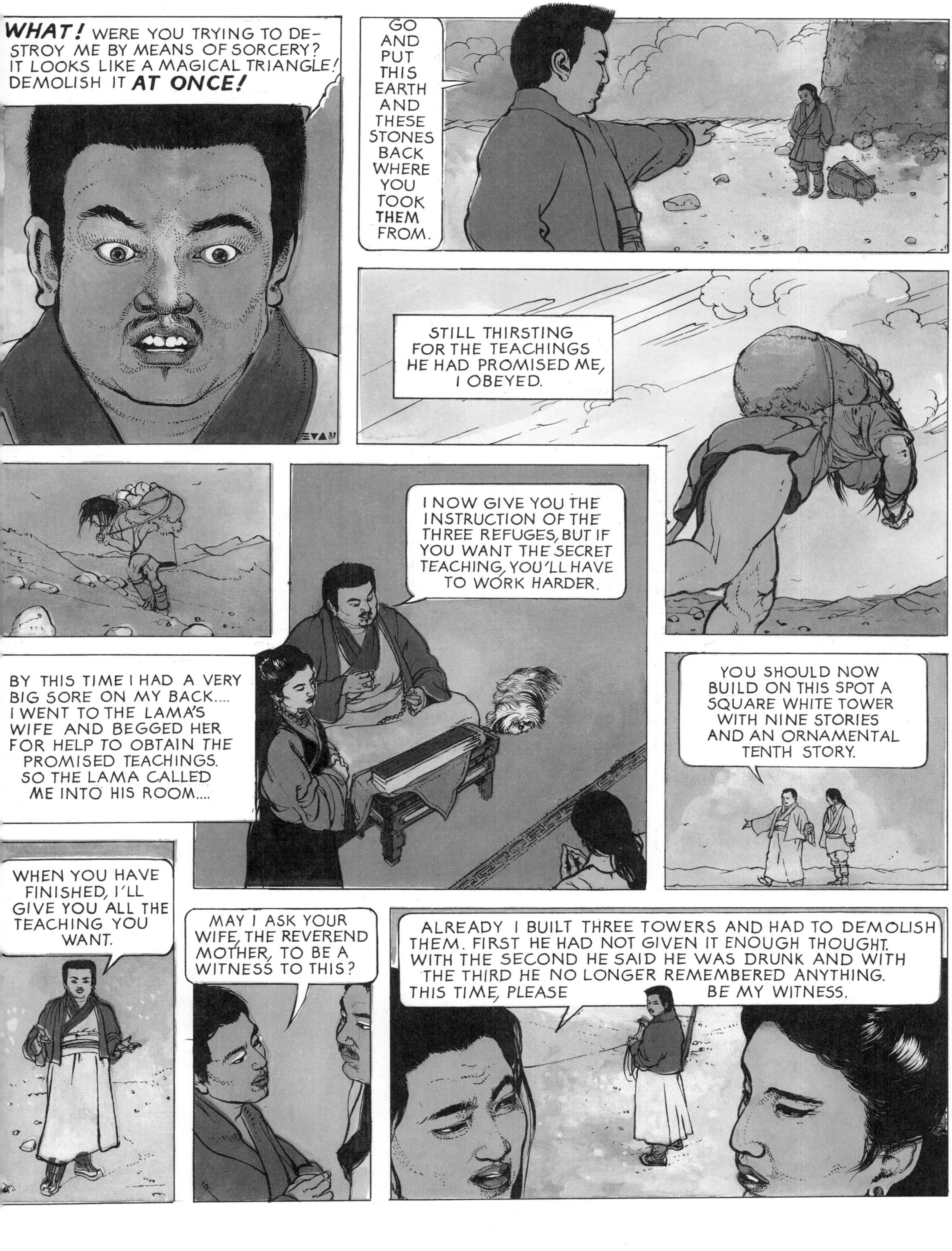
WHAT! WERE YOU TRYING TO DESTROY ME BY MEANS OF SORCERY? IT LOOKS LIKE A MAGICAL TRIANGLE! DEMOLISH IT AT ONCE!
GO AND PUT THIS EARTH AND THESE STONES BACK WHERE YOU TOOK THEM FROM.
STILL THIRSTING FOR THE TEACHINGS HE HAD PROMISED ME, I OBEYED.
I NOW GIVE YOU THE INSTRUCTION OF THE THREE REFUGES, BUT IF YOU WANT THE SECRET TEACHING, YOU'LL HAVE TO WORK HARDER.
BY THIS TIME I HAD A VERY BIG SORE ON MY BACK.... I WENT TO THE LAMA'S WIFE AND BEGGED HER FOR HELP TO OBTAIN THE PROMISED TEACHINGS. SO THE LAMA CALLED ME INTO HIS ROOM....
YOU SHOULD NOW BUILD ON THIS SPOT A SQUARE WHITE TOWER WITH NINE STORIES AND AN ORNAMENTAL TENTH STORY.
WHEN YOU HAVE FINISHED, I'LL GIVE YOU ALL THE TEACHING YOU WANT.
MAY I ASK YOUR WIFE, THE REVEREND MOTHER, TO BE A WITNESS TO THIS?
ALREADY I BUILT THREE TOWERS AND HAD TO DEMOLISH THEM. FIRST HE HAD NOT GIVEN IT ENOUGH THOUGHT. WITH THE SECOND HE SAID HE WAS DRUNK AND WITH THE THIRD HE NO LONGER REMEMBERED ANYTHING. THIS TIME, PLEASE BE MY WITNESS.

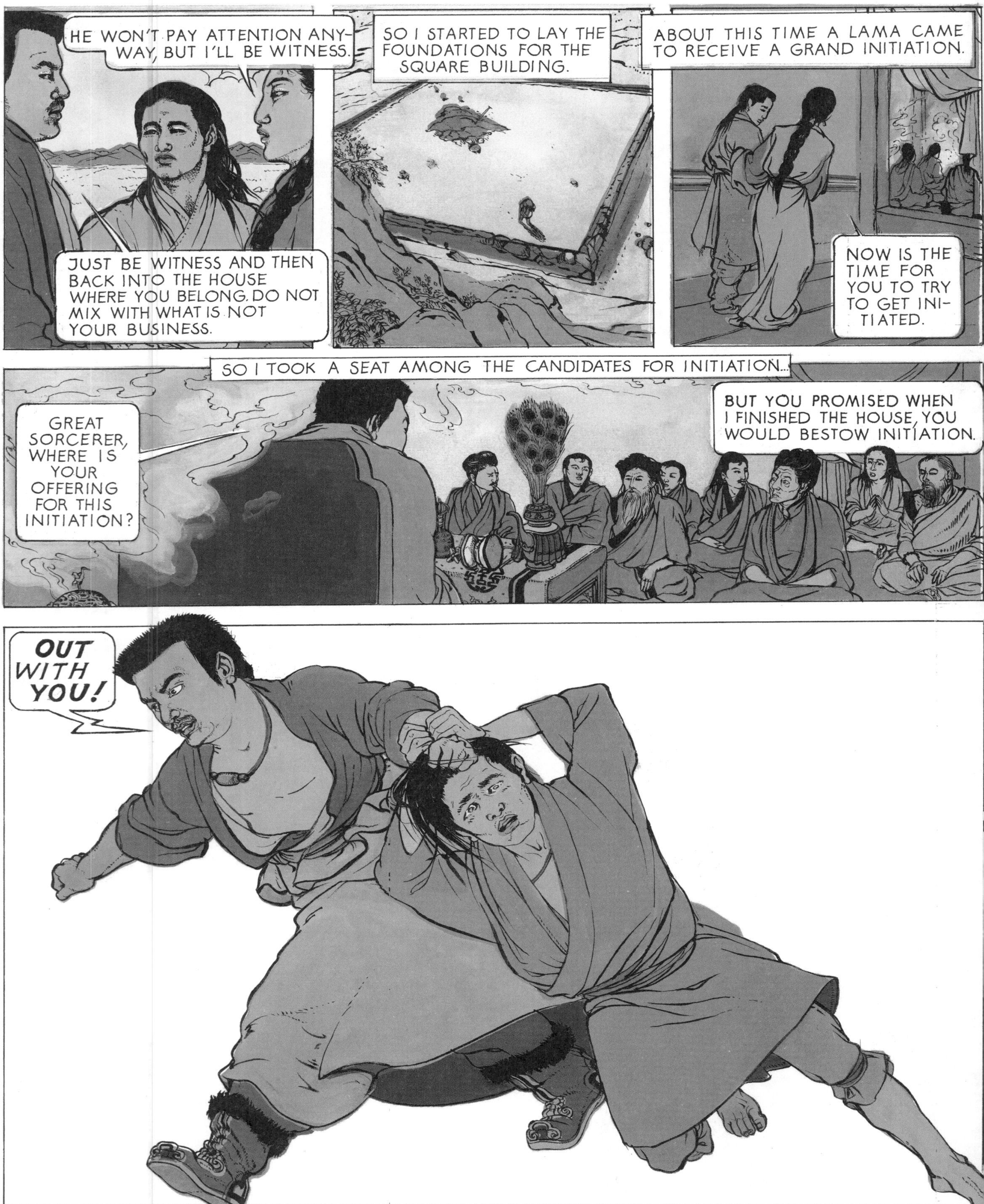
HE WON'T PAY ATTENTION ANYWAY, BUT I'LL BE WITNESS.
JUST BE WITNESS AND THEN BACK INTO THE HOUSE WHERE YOU BELONG. DO NOT MIX WITH WHAT IS NOT YOUR BUSINESS.
SO I STARTED TO LAY THE FOUNDATIONS FOR THE SQUARE BUILDING.
ABOUT THIS TIME A LAMA CAME TO RECEIVE A GRAND INITIATION.
NOW IS THE TIME FOR YOU TO TRY TO GET INITIATED.
SO I TOOK A SEAT AMONG THE CANDIDATES FOR INITIATION...
BUT YOU PROMISED WHEN I FINISHED THE HOUSE, YOU WOULD BESTOW INITIATION.
GREAT SORCERER, WHERE IS YOUR OFFERING FOR THIS INITIATION?
OUT WITH YOU!

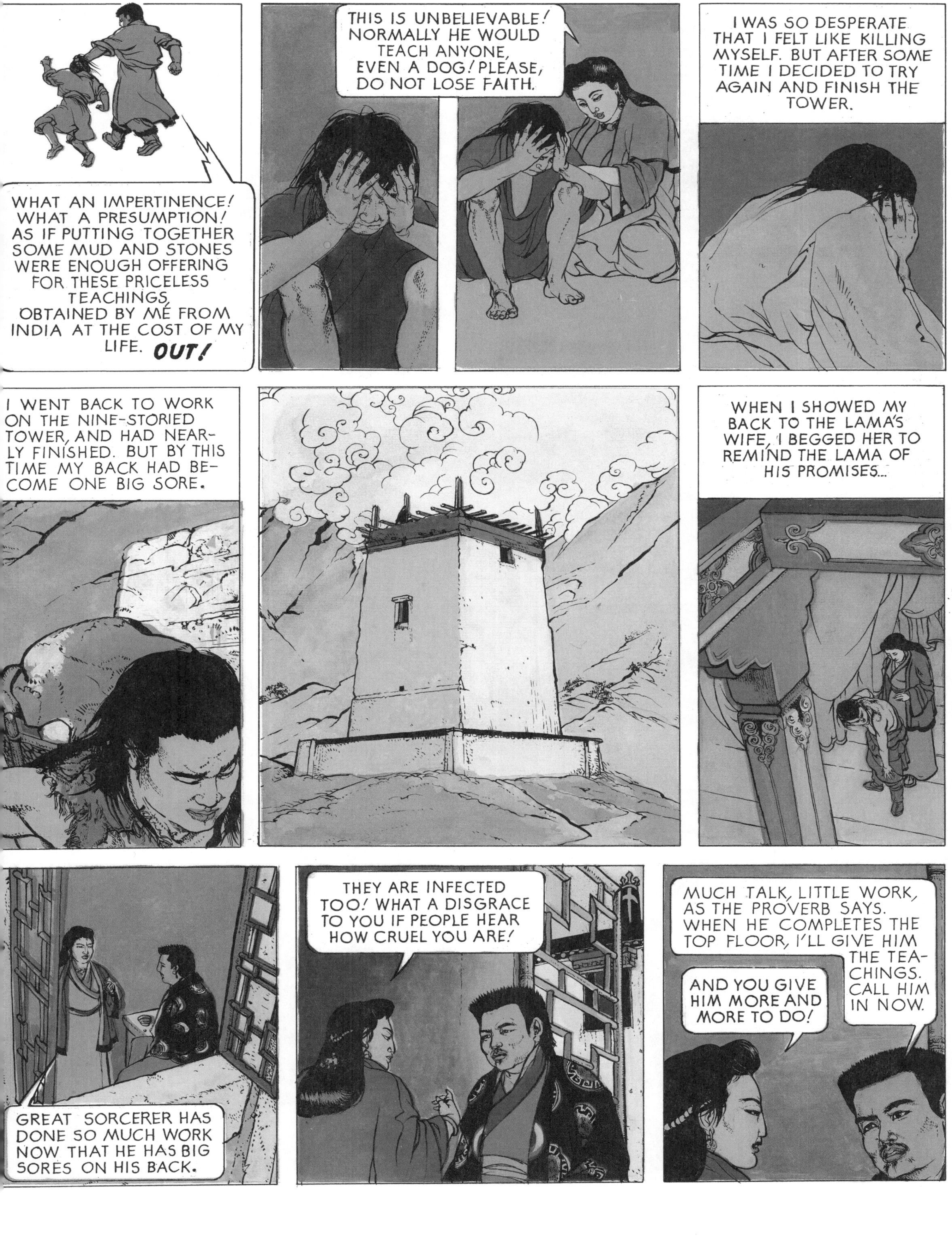
WHAT AN IMPERTINENCE! WHAT A PRESUMPTION! AS IF PUTTING TOGETHER SOME MUD AND STONES WERE ENOUGH OFFERING FOR THESE PRICELESS TEACHINGS, OBTAINED BY ME FROM INDIA AT THE COST OF MY LIFE. OUT!
THIS IS UNBELIEVABLE! NORMALLY HE WOULD TEACH ANYONE, EVEN A DOG! PLEASE, DO NOT LOSE FAITH.
I WAS SO DESPERATE THAT I FELT LIKE KILLING MYSELF. BUT AFTER SOME TIME I DECIDED TO TRY AGAIN AND FINISH THE TOWER.
I WENT BACK TO WORK ON THE NINE-STORIED TOWER, AND HAD NEARLY FINISHED. BUT BY THIS TIME MY BACK HAD BECOME ONE BIG SORE.
WHEN I SHOWED MY BACK TO THE LAMA'S WIFE, I BEGGED HER TO REMIND THE LAMA OF HIS PROMISES...
GREAT SORCERER HAS DONE SO MUCH WORK NOW THAT HE HAS BIG SORES ON HIS BACK.
THEY ARE INFECTED TOO! WHAT A DISGRACE TO YOU IF PEOPLE HEAR HOW CRUEL YOU ARE!
MUCH TALK, LITTLE WORK, AS THE PROVERB SAYS. WHEN HE COMPLETES THE TOP FLOOR, I'LL GIVE HIM THE TEACHINGS. CALL HIM IN NOW.
AND YOU GIVE HIM MORE AND MORE TO DO!

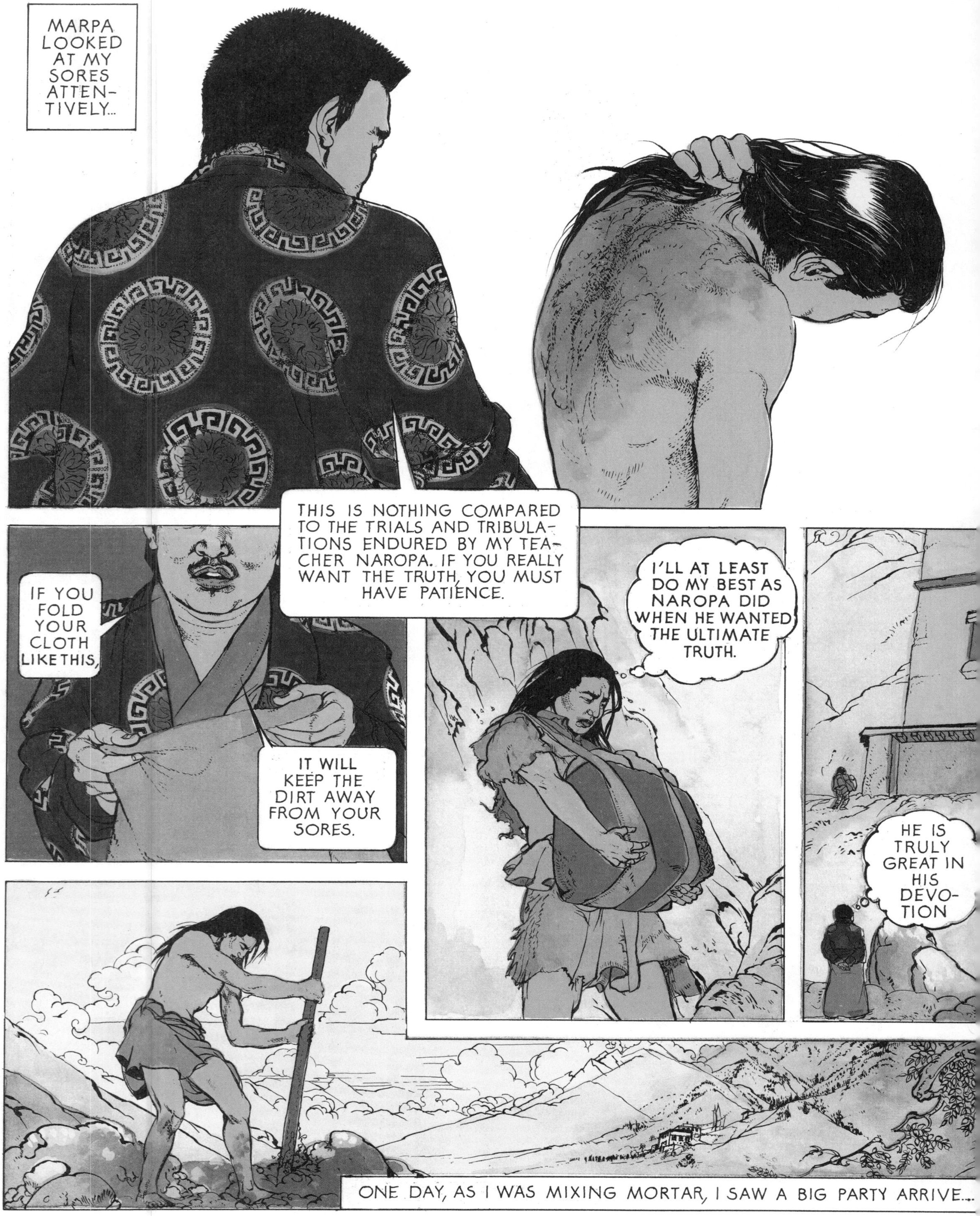
MARPA LOOKED AT MY SORES ATTENTIVELY...
THIS IS NOTHING COMPARED TO THE TRIALS AND TRIBULATIONS ENDURED BY MY TEACHER NAROPA. IF YOU REALLY WANT THE TRUTH, YOU MUST HAVE PATIENCE.
IF YOU FOLD YOUR CLOTH LIKE THIS,
IT WILL KEEP THE DIRT AWAY FROM YOUR SORES.
I'LL AT LEAST DO MY BEST AS NAROPA DID WHEN HE WANTED THE ULTIMATE TRUTH.
HE IS TRULY GREAT IN HIS DEVOTION
ONE DAY, AS I WAS MIXING MORTAR, I SAW A BIG PARTY ARRIVE...

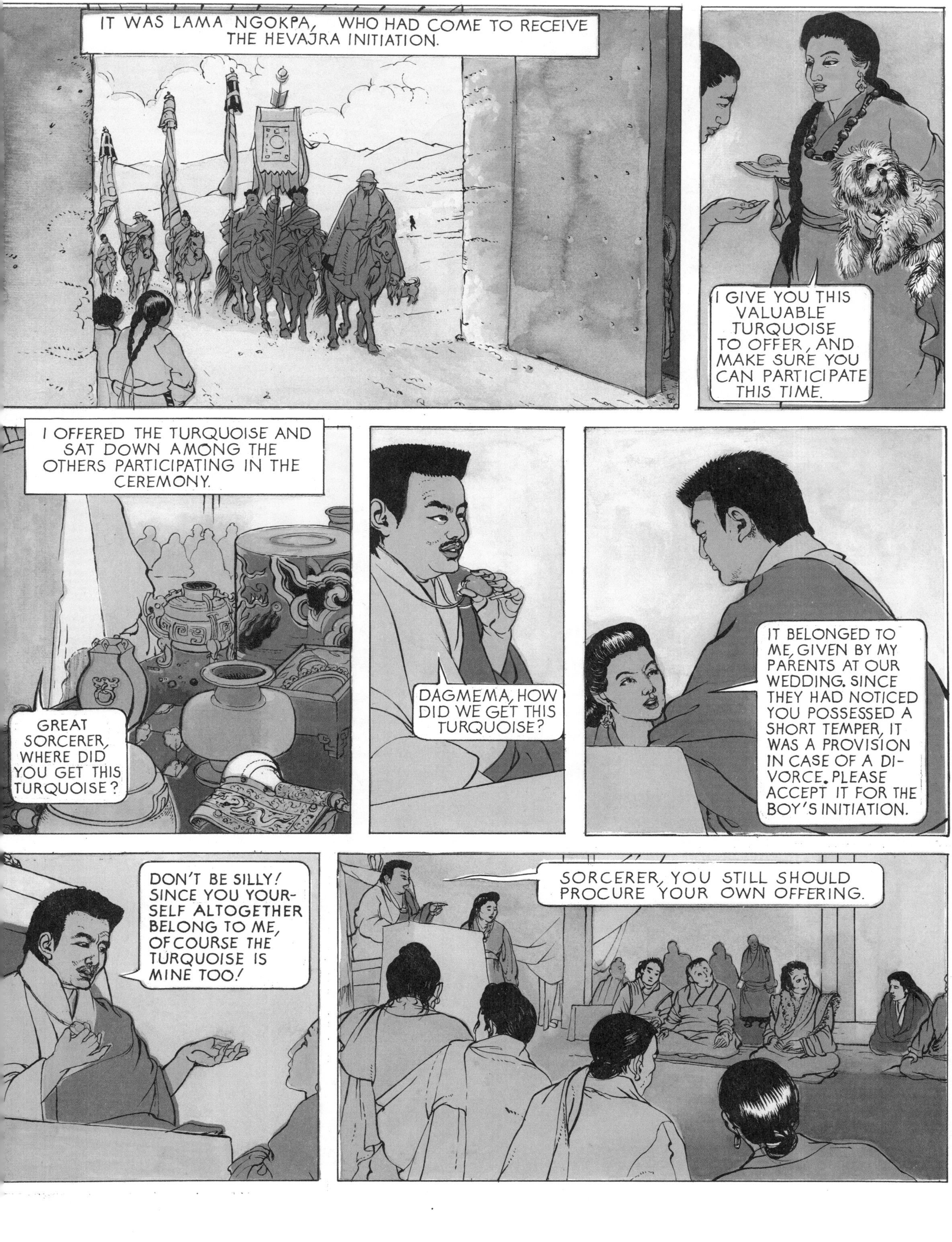
IT WAS LAMA NGOKPA, WHO HAD COME TO RECEIVE THE HEVAJRA INITIATION.
I GIVE YOU THIS VALUABLE TURQUOISE TO OFFER, AND MAKE SURE YOU CAN PARTICIPATE THIS TIME.
I OFFERED THE TURQUOISE AND SAT DOWN AMONG THE OTHERS PARTICIPATING IN THE CEREMONY.
GREAT SORCERER, WHERE DID YOU GET THIS TURQUOISE?
DAGMEMA, HOW DID WE GET THIS TURQUOISE?
IT BELONGED TO ME, GIVEN BY MY PARENTS AT OUR WEDDING. SINCE THEY HAD NOTICED YOU POSSESSED A SHORT TEMPER, IT WAS A PROVISION IN CASE OF A DI-VORCE. PLEASE ACCEPT IT FOR THE BOY'S INITIATION.
DON'T BE SILLY! SINCE YOU YOUR-SELF ALTOGETHER BELONG TO ME, OF COURSE THE TURQUOISE IS MINE TOO!
SORCERER, YOU STILL SHOULD PROCURE YOUR OWN OFFERING.

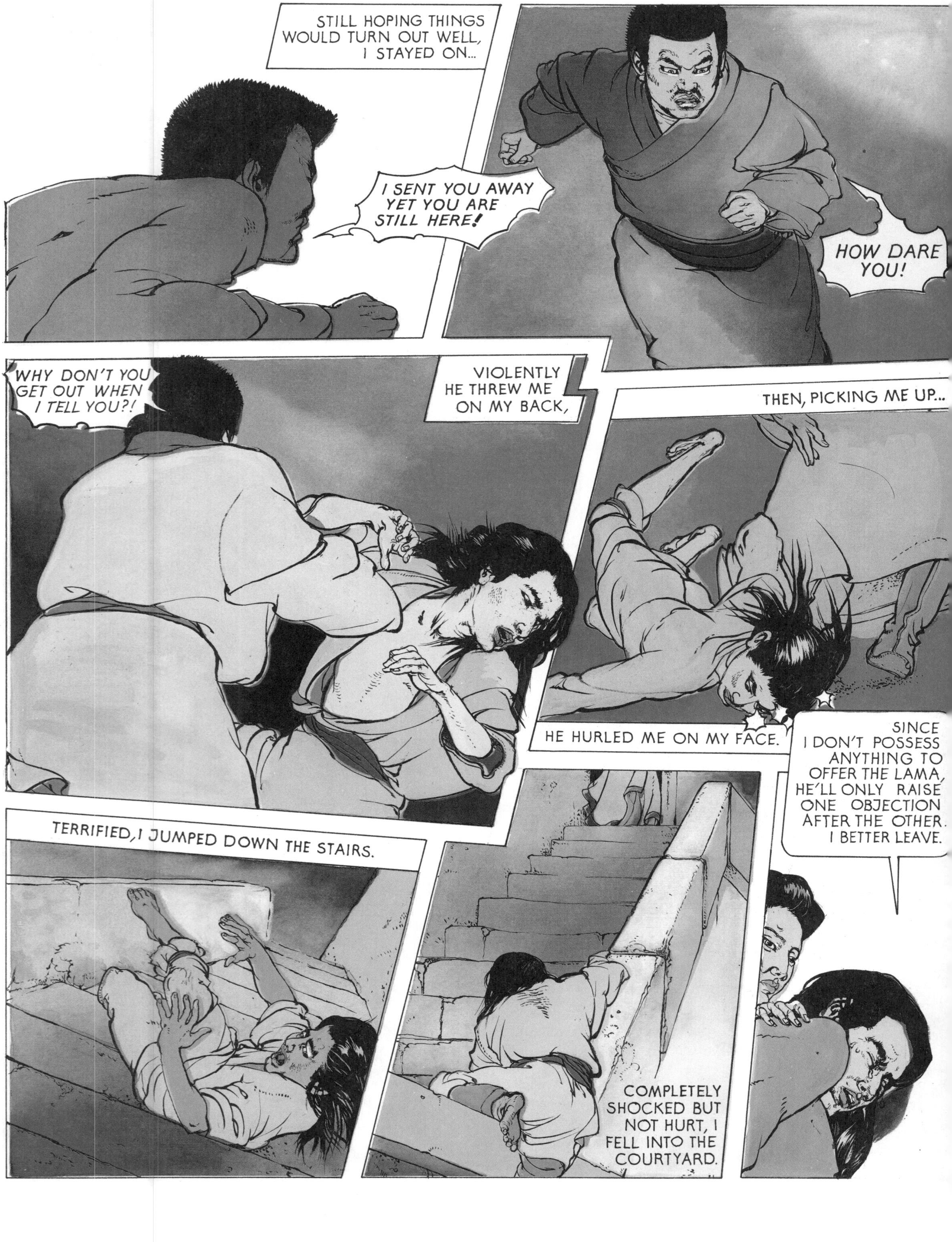
STILL HOPING THINGS WOULD TURN OUT WELL, I STAYED ON...
I SENT YOU AWAY YET YOU ARE STILL HERE!
HOW DARE YOU!
WHY DON'T YOU GET OUT WHEN I TELL YOU?!
VIOLENTLY HE THREW ME ON MY BACK,
THEN, PICKING ME UP...
HE HURLED ME ON MY FACE.
TERRIFIED, I JUMPED DOWN THE STAIRS.
COMPLETELY SHOCKED BUT NOT HURT, I FELL INTO THE COURTYARD.
SINCE I DON'T POSSESS ANYTHING TO OFFER THE LAMA, HE'LL ONLY RAISE ONE OBJECTION AFTER THE OTHER. I BETTER LEAVE.

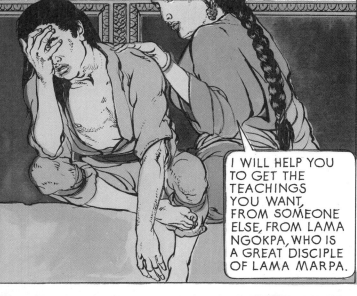

I WILL HELP YOU TO GET THE TEACHINGS YOU WANT, FROM SOMEONE ELSE, FROM LAMA NGOKPA, WHO IS A GREAT DISCIPLE OF LAMA MARPA.

DAGMEMA BREWED A STRONG BEER TO BE SERVED AT THE TENTH DAY OF THE MOON-CELEBRATIONS. MARPA AND THE OTHER YOGIS WERE SERVED BY HER WITH LARGE QUANTITIES OF THE STRONGEST BREW...

NOW IS THE TIME!

COMPLETELY DRUNK, THEY FELL INTO A DEEP SLEEP....

I'LL TAKE THESE RELICS OF NAROPA FROM HIS CABINET AND WRITE A LETTER TO GO WITH IT.

WHEN YOU OFFER THIS TO LAMA NGOKPA,

ACT AS IF IT WERE SENT BY MARPA HIMSELF.

WITH NAROPA'S RELICS AND THE LETTER WITH MARPA'S SEAL ON IT, I SET OUT FOR LAMA NGOKPA'S RESIDENCE.

ARE YOU SATISFIED NOW? YOUR GREAT ENEMY HAS LEFT YOU. SINCE HE GOT ONLY SCOLDINGS AND BEATINGS, HE WANTED TO LOOK FOR A GURU ELSEWHERE...

O GURUS AND PROTECTORS! PLEASE BRING BACK MY DESTINED DISCIPLE!

LAMA NGOKPA WAS OVERJOYED WHEN I HANDED HIM THE GIFTS...

AH! MY HUMBLE MONASTERY TO BE BLESSED AND **HONORED** WITH SUCH PRECIOUS RELICS OF THE GREAT TEACHER NAROPA!

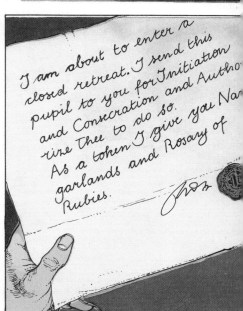

I am about to enter a closed retreat. I send this pupil to you for Initiation and Consecration and Authorize Thee to do so. As a token I give you Naropa's garlands and Rosary of Rubies.

AFTER THIS LAMA NGOKPA GAVE ME THE INITIATION. I MADE A CAVE INHABITABLE AND SPENT MY TIME IN MEDITATION.

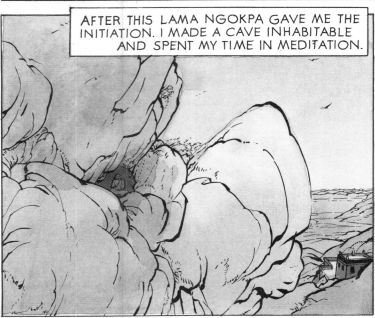

HOWEVER, NO EXPERIENCES OF ANY KIND AROSE...

HOW IS THIS POSSIBLE? IN THIS LINE OF DEVELOPMENT THERE OUGHT TO BE SIGNS...

THERE MUST BE SOMETHING DIRECTLY IN THE WAY. WHAT COULD IT BE?

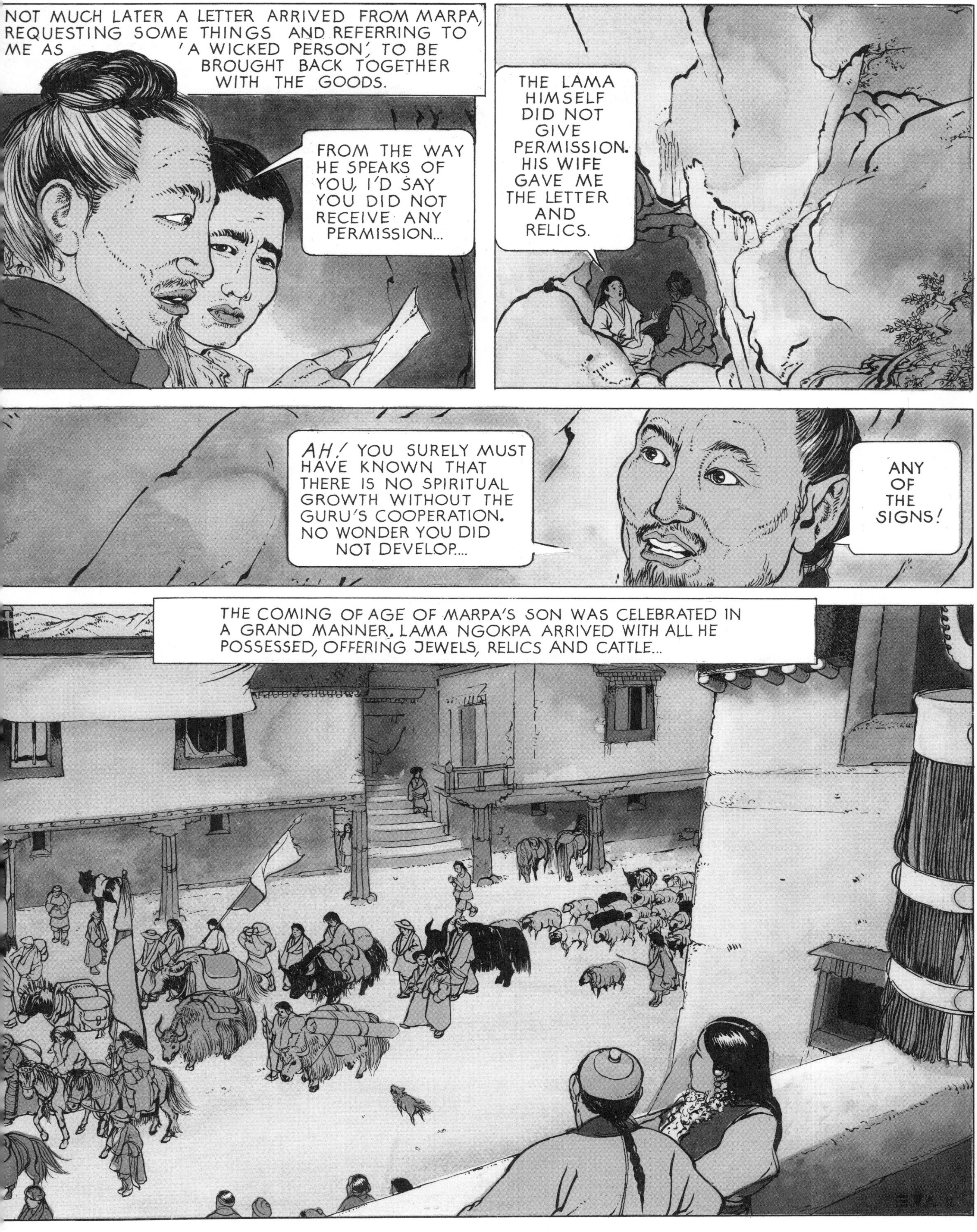
NOT MUCH LATER A LETTER ARRIVED FROM MARPA, REQUESTING SOME THINGS AND REFERRING TO ME AS 'A WICKED PERSON,' TO BE BROUGHT BACK TOGETHER WITH THE GOODS.
FROM THE WAY HE SPEAKS OF YOU, I'D SAY YOU DID NOT RECEIVE ANY PERMISSION...
THE LAMA HIMSELF DID NOT GIVE PERMISSION. HIS WIFE GAVE ME THE LETTER AND RELICS.
AH! YOU SURELY MUST HAVE KNOWN THAT THERE IS NO SPIRITUAL GROWTH WITHOUT THE GURU'S COOPERATION. NO WONDER YOU DID NOT DEVELOP...
ANY OF THE SIGNS!
THE COMING OF AGE OF MARPA'S SON WAS CELEBRATED IN A GRAND MANNER. LAMA NGOKPA ARRIVED WITH ALL HE POSSESSED, OFFERING JEWELS, RELICS AND CATTLE...

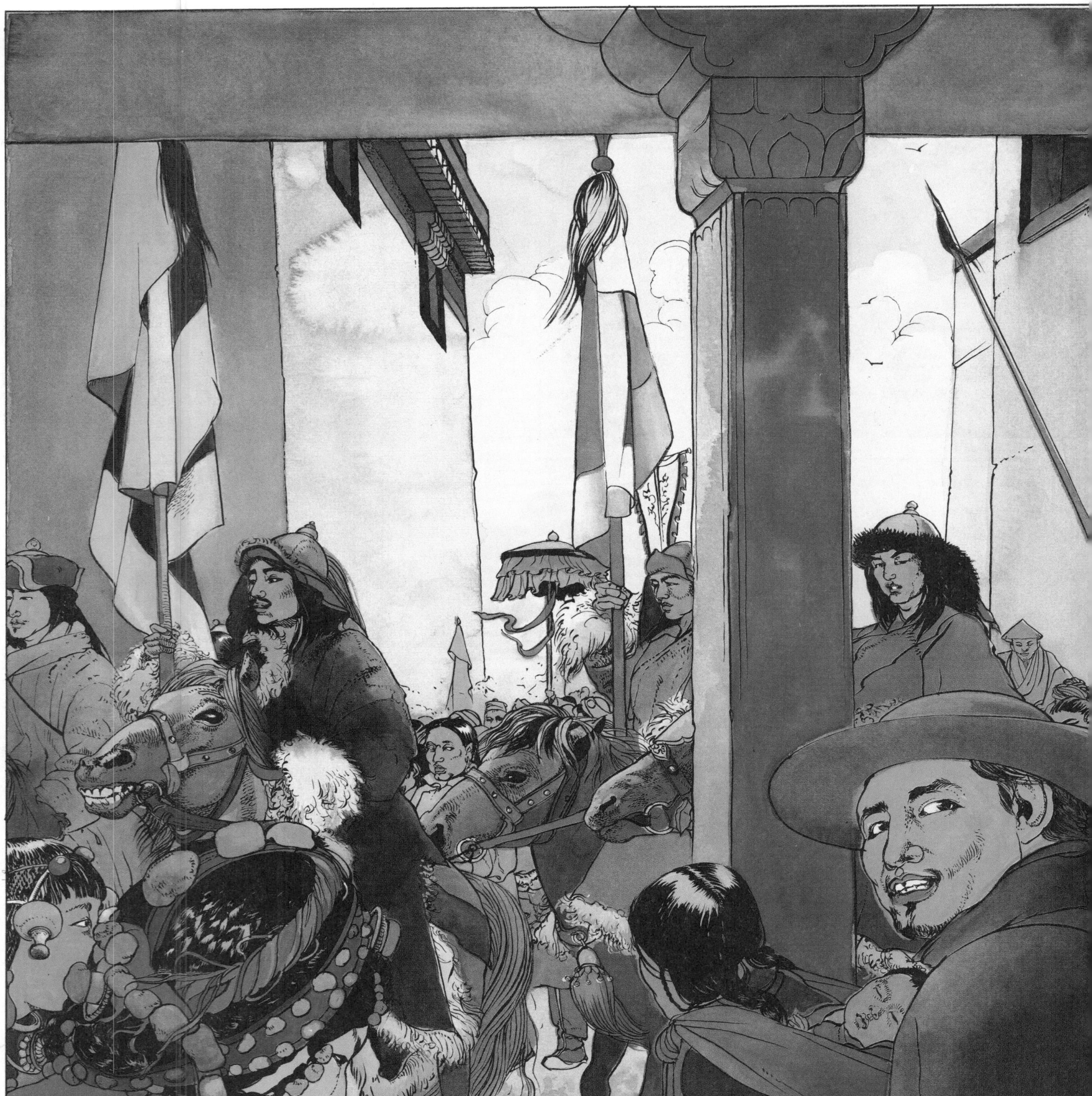

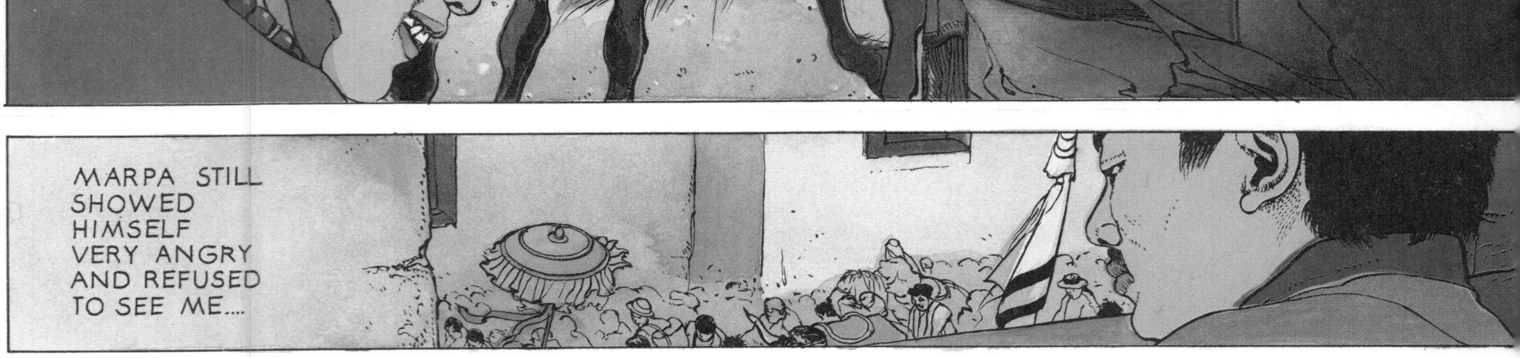
MARPA STILL SHOWED HIMSELF VERY ANGRY AND REFUSED TO SEE ME....

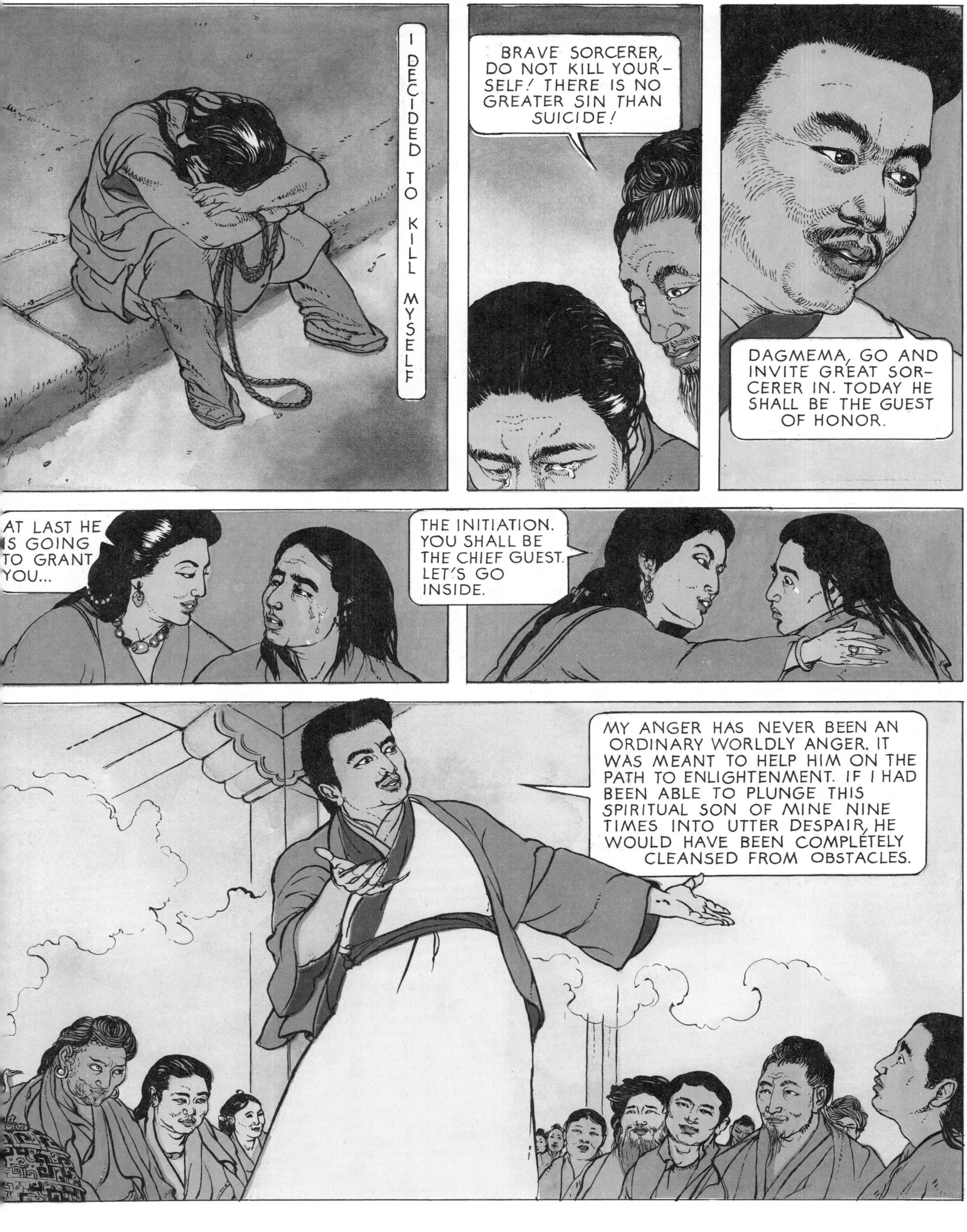
I DECIDED TO KILL MYSELF
BRAVE SORCERER, DO NOT KILL YOURSELF! THERE IS NO GREATER SIN THAN SUICIDE!
DAGMEMA, GO AND INVITE GREAT SORCERER IN. TODAY HE SHALL BE THE GUEST OF HONOR.
AT LAST HE IS GOING TO GRANT YOU...
THE INITIATION. YOU SHALL BE THE CHIEF GUEST. LET'S GO INSIDE.
MY ANGER HAS NEVER BEEN AN ORDINARY WORLDLY ANGER. IT WAS MEANT TO HELP HIM ON THE PATH TO ENLIGHTENMENT. IF I HAD BEEN ABLE TO PLUNGE THIS SPIRITUAL SON OF MINE NINE TIMES INTO UTTER DESPAIR, HE WOULD HAVE BEEN COMPLETELY CLEANSED FROM OBSTACLES.

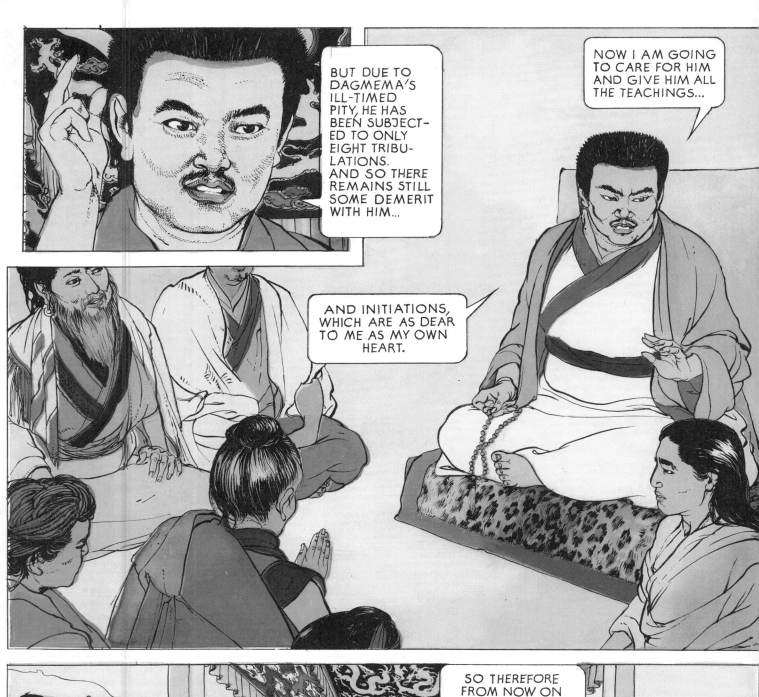

BUT DUE TO DAGMEMA'S ILL-TIMED PITY, HE HAS BEEN SUBJECTED TO ONLY EIGHT TRIBULATIONS. AND SO THERE REMAINS STILL SOME DEMERIT WITH HIM...

NOW I AM GOING TO CARE FOR HIM AND GIVE HIM ALL THE TEACHINGS...

AND INITIATIONS, WHICH ARE AS DEAR TO ME AS MY OWN HEART.

SO THEREFORE FROM NOW ON *REJOICE!*

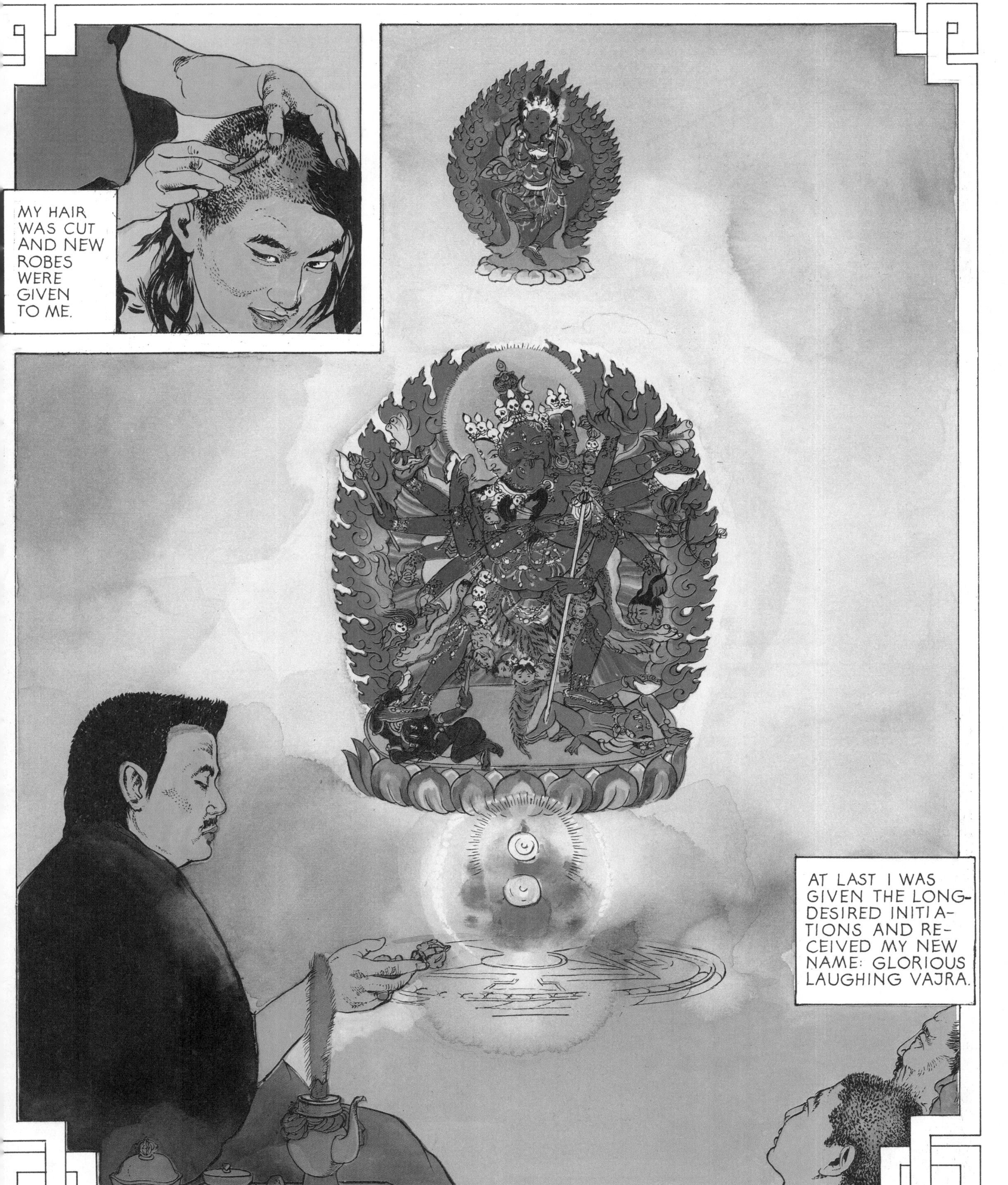
MY HAIR WAS CUT AND NEW ROBES WERE GIVEN TO ME.
AT LAST I WAS GIVEN THE LONG-DESIRED INITIATIONS AND RECEIVED MY NEW NAME: GLORIOUS LAUGHING VAJRA.

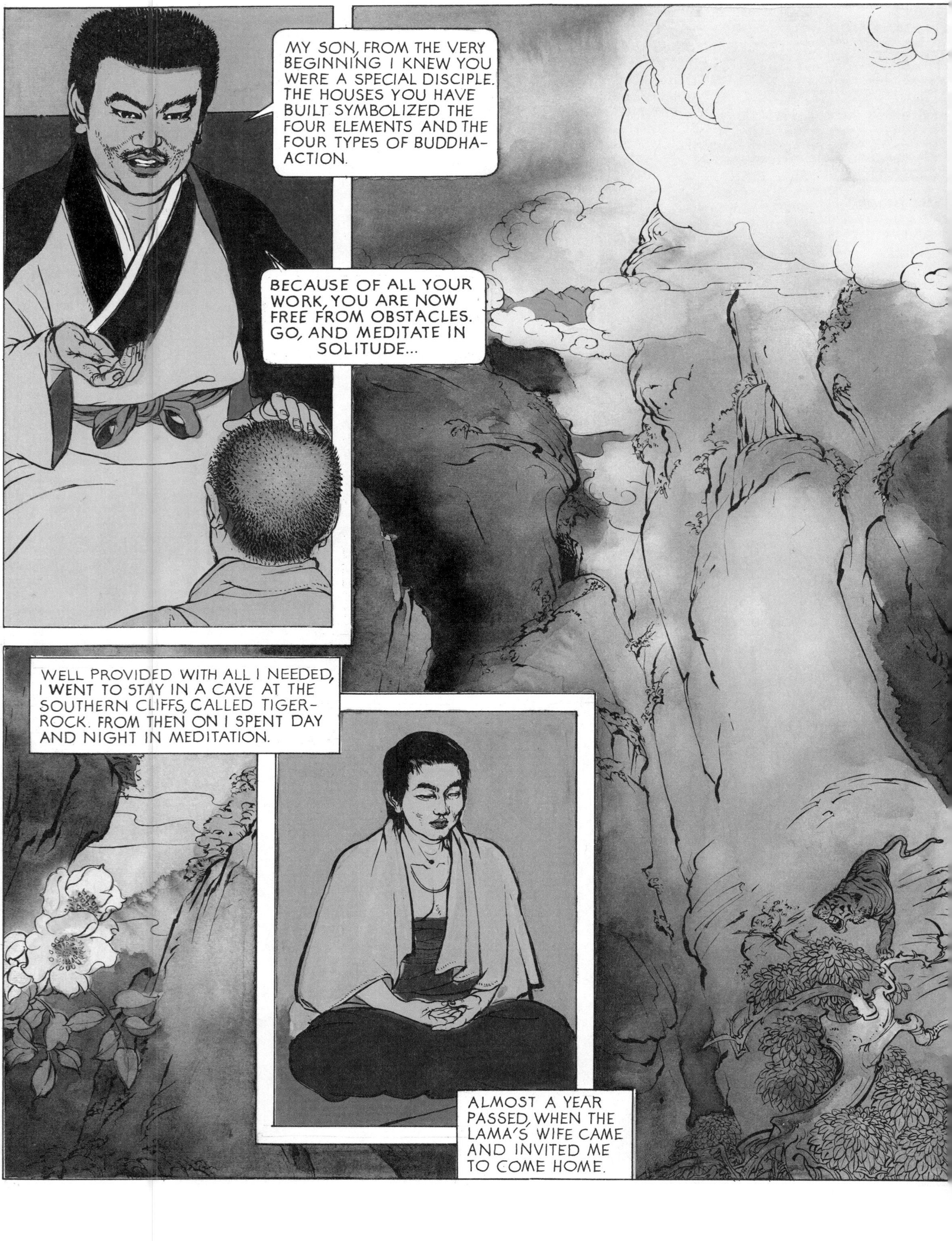
MY SON, FROM THE VERY BEGINNING I KNEW YOU WERE A SPECIAL DISCIPLE. THE HOUSES YOU HAVE BUILT SYMBOLIZED THE FOUR ELEMENTS AND THE FOUR TYPES OF BUDDHA-ACTION.
BECAUSE OF ALL YOUR WORK, YOU ARE NOW FREE FROM OBSTACLES. GO, AND MEDITATE IN SOLITUDE...
WELL PROVIDED WITH ALL I NEEDED, I WENT TO STAY IN A CAVE AT THE SOUTHERN CLIFFS, CALLED TIGER-ROCK. FROM THEN ON I SPENT DAY AND NIGHT IN MEDITATION.
ALMOST A YEAR PASSED, WHEN THE LAMA'S WIFE CAME AND INVITED ME TO COME HOME.

THEN MARPA ASKED ME TO TELL ABOUT MY EXPERIENCES AND UNDERSTANDING.

I HAVE UNDERSTOOD THAT THIS BODY ALONG WITH CONSCIOUSNESS IS GATHERED BY THE TWELVE INTER-DEPENDENT LINKS, ORIGINATING FROM IGNORANCE. I RELY UPON YOUR POWER OF COMPASSION AS MY GUIDE TO ATTAIN LIBERATION FROM THE ENDLESS EXISTENTIAL SUFFERING. IT IS YOU WHO GAVE ME INITIATION INTO ULTIMATE REALITY. THIS MEDITATOR HAS DISCOVERED THE NON-EXISTENCE OF A PERSONAL SELF, AND CAN SO ATTAIN PURE CONSCIOUSNESS, NAKED, SHARP AND VIVID. **THEREFORE** I WILL GO THROUGH THE STAGES OF ATTAINING PERFECT INSIGHT AND AROUSING COMPASSION, THROUGH PERFECT SEEING, REACH THE NON-CONCEPTUAL STATE. THEN, REALIZING VOIDNESS, I DEDICATE THE RESULTS FOR THE BENEFIT OF OTHERS. I OFFER TO YOU THE BEST OF MY ATTAINMENTS AS A MEDITATOR, AS LONG AS I LIVE.

MY SON, I HAD HIGH EXPECTATIONS OF YOU AND THEY HAVE BEEN FULFILLED!

AFTER THIS I WENT BACK TO THE CAVE IN THE HILLS BEHIND THE MONASTERY AND STAYED IN MEDITATION.

MARPA WENT ON ANOTHER JOURNEY TO INDIA TO SEE HIS TEACHER NAROPA ONCE MORE. AT HIS RETURN ALL HIS DISCIPLES ASSEMBLED.

I AM GETTING OLD AND WOULD LIKE TO ENSURE THAT THIS LINE OF TEACHINGS REMAINS UNBROKEN; I HAVE THE POWER OF **PROPHECY** THROUGH DREAMS AND OMENS. YOU DISCIPLES GO AND REPORT TO ME THE DREAMS YOU HAVE.

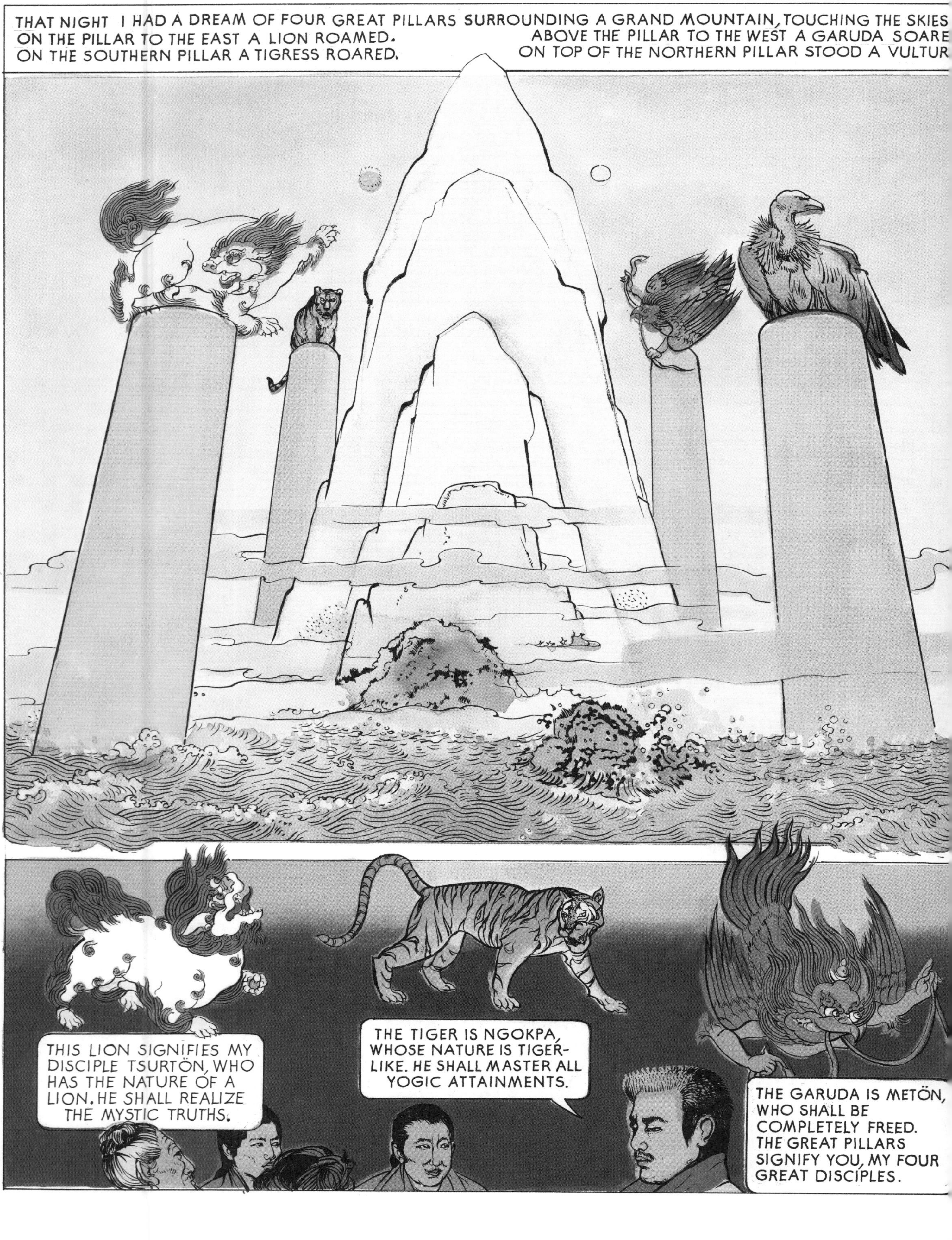
THAT NIGHT I HAD A DREAM OF FOUR GREAT PILLARS SURROUNDING A GRAND MOUNTAIN, TOUCHING THE SKIES
ON THE PILLAR TO THE EAST A LION ROAMED.
ON THE SOUTHERN PILLAR A TIGRESS ROARED.
ABOVE THE PILLAR TO THE WEST A GARUDA SOARE
ON TOP OF THE NORTHERN PILLAR STOOD A VULTUR
THIS LION SIGNIFIES MY DISCIPLE TSURTÖN, WHO HAS THE NATURE OF A LION. HE SHALL REALIZE THE MYSTIC TRUTHS.
THE TIGER IS NGOKPA, WHOSE NATURE IS TIGER-LIKE. HE SHALL MASTER ALL YOGIC ATTAINMENTS.
THE GARUDA IS METÖN, WHO SHALL BE COMPLETELY FREED. THE GREAT PILLARS SIGNIFY YOU, MY FOUR GREAT DISCIPLES.

THE GREAT PILLAR TO THE NORTH IS MILAREPA. THE VULTURE ABOVE IT SHOWS HIM TO BE IN NATURE VULTURE-LIKE, ENDOWED WITH THE MYSTIC TRUTHS...

AND ENDURING LIKE A ROCK. THIS DREAM IS EXCELLENT AND HOLDS THE PROPHECY THAT THIS LINEAGE WILL BE GLORIOUS.

MARPA OPENED FOR US HIS TREASURES OF SACRED SCROLLS AND BOOKS ON MYSTIC TRUTHS AND SCIENCES, AND EXPLAINED THEM TO US.

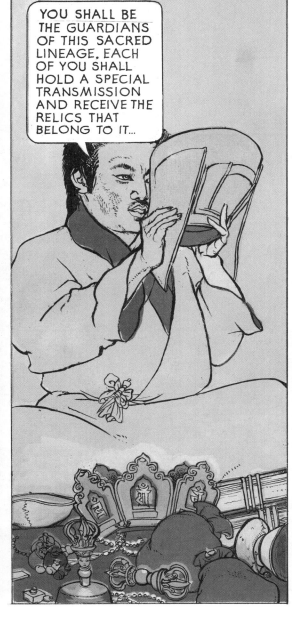

YOU SHALL BE THE GUARDIANS OF THIS SACRED LINEAGE. EACH OF YOU SHALL HOLD A SPECIAL TRANSMISSION AND RECEIVE THE RELICS THAT BELONG TO IT...

MARPA GAVE ME THE TEXT ON THE SCIENCE OF INNER HEAT, WHICH ALLOWS ONE TO LIVE IN SOLITUDE ABOVE THE SNOWLINE.

STAY A FEW YEARS LONGER NEAR ME. I HAVE SEVERAL MORE TEACHINGS AND INITIATIONS TO GIVE TO YOU.

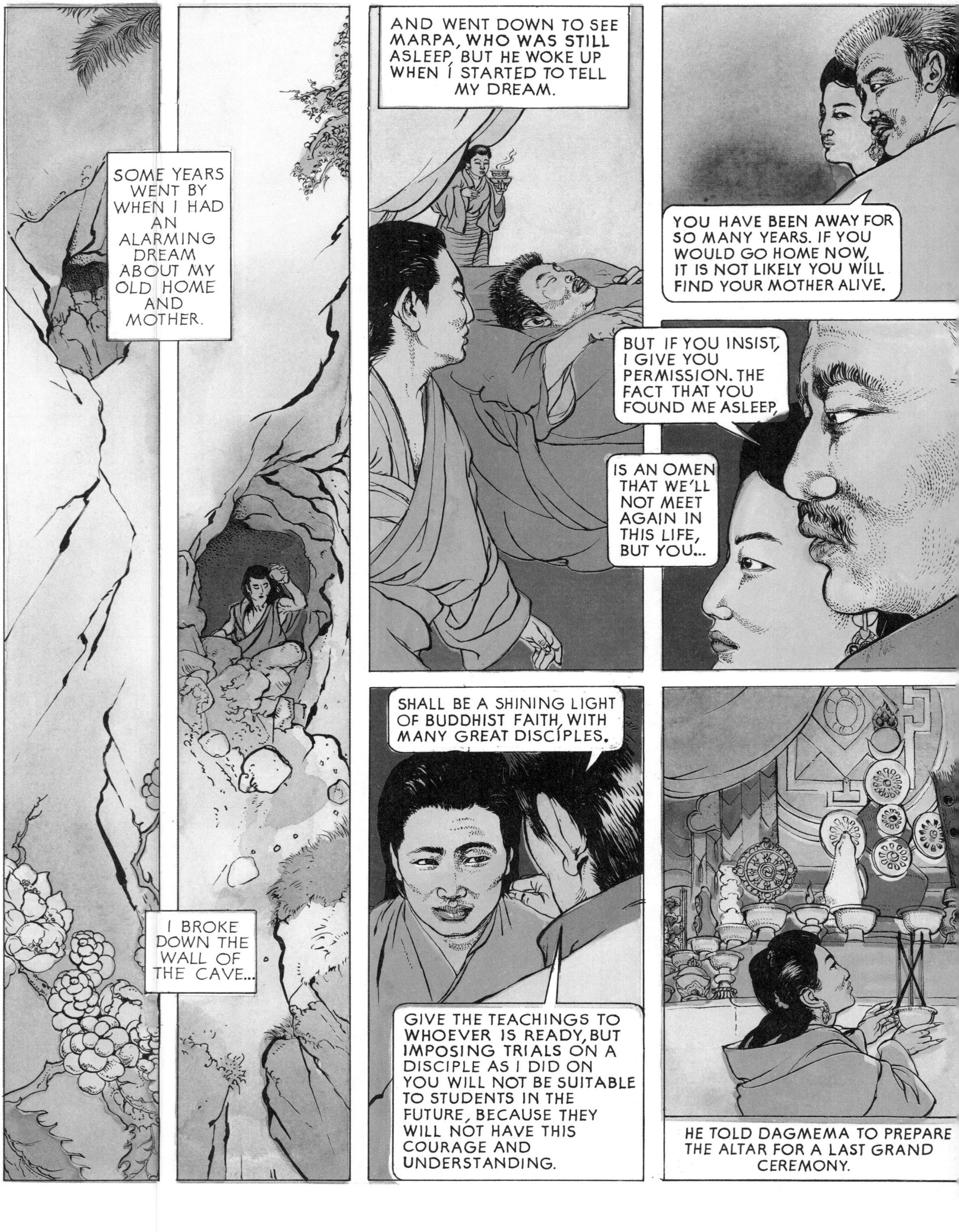
SOME YEARS WENT BY WHEN I HAD AN ALARMING DREAM ABOUT MY OLD HOME AND MOTHER.
I BROKE DOWN THE WALL OF THE CAVE...
AND WENT DOWN TO SEE MARPA, WHO WAS STILL ASLEEP, BUT HE WOKE UP WHEN I STARTED TO TELL MY DREAM.
YOU HAVE BEEN AWAY FOR SO MANY YEARS. IF YOU WOULD GO HOME NOW, IT IS NOT LIKELY YOU WILL FIND YOUR MOTHER ALIVE.
BUT IF YOU INSIST, I GIVE YOU PERMISSION. THE FACT THAT YOU FOUND ME ASLEEP,
IS AN OMEN THAT WE'LL NOT MEET AGAIN IN THIS LIFE, BUT YOU...
SHALL BE A SHINING LIGHT OF BUDDHIST FAITH, WITH MANY GREAT DISCIPLES.
GIVE THE TEACHINGS TO WHOEVER IS READY, BUT IMPOSING TRIALS ON A DISCIPLE AS I DID ON YOU WILL NOT BE SUITABLE TO STUDENTS IN THE FUTURE, BECAUSE THEY WILL NOT HAVE THIS COURAGE AND UNDERSTANDING.
HE TOLD DAGMEMA TO PREPARE THE ALTAR FOR A LAST GRAND CEREMONY.

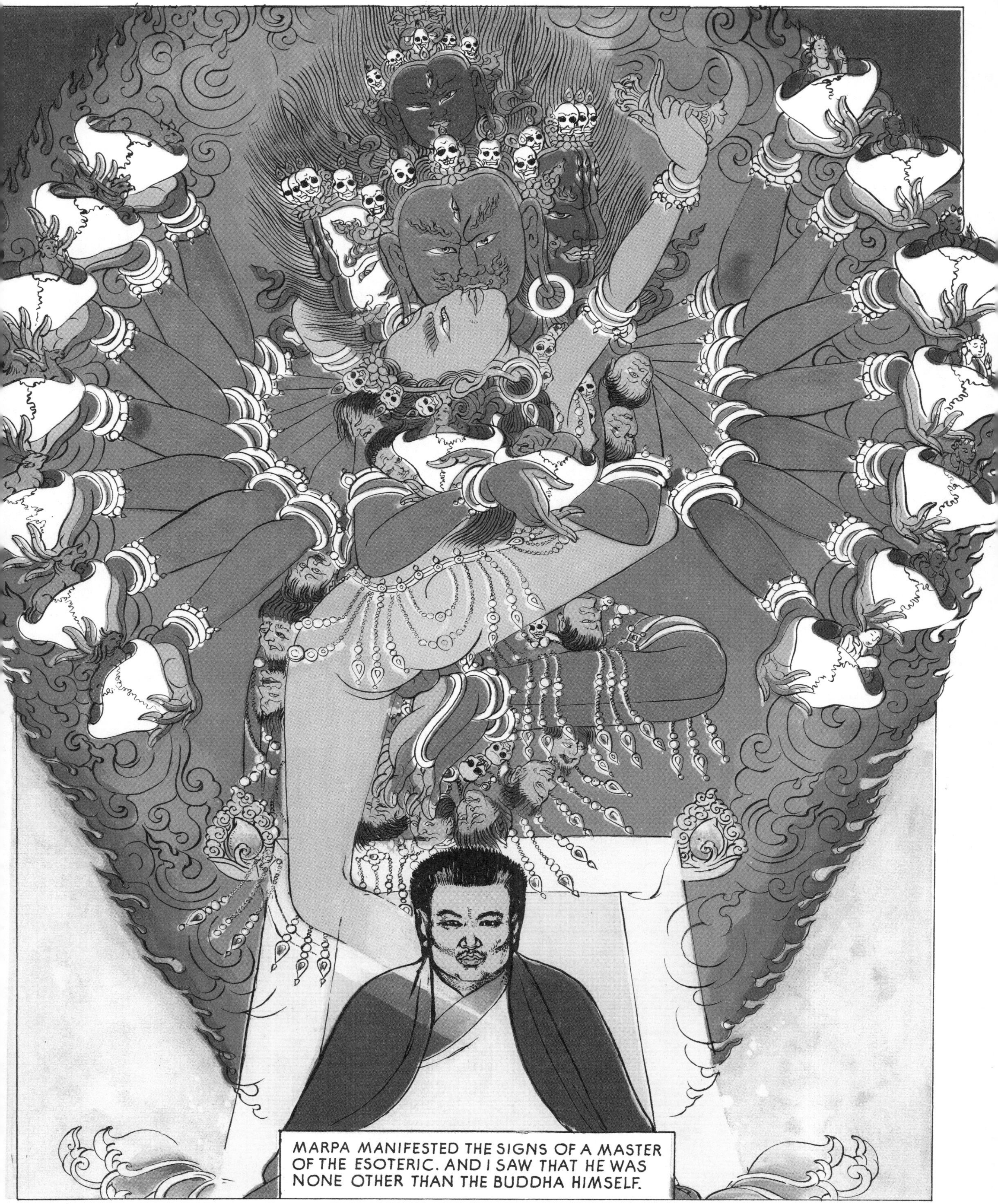
MARPA MANIFESTED THE SIGNS OF A MASTER OF THE ESOTERIC. AND I SAW THAT HE WAS NONE OTHER THAN THE BUDDHA HIMSELF.

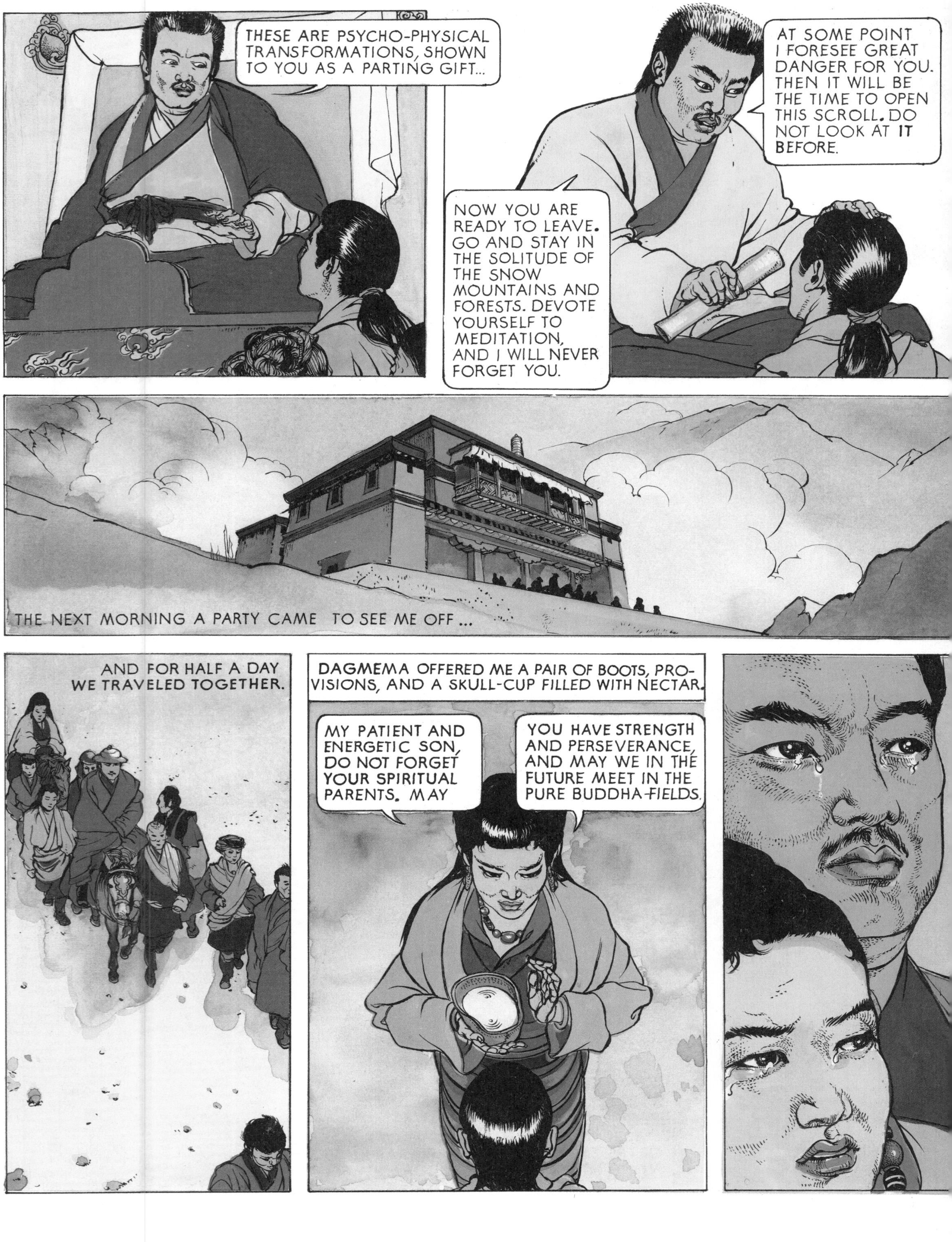
THESE ARE PSYCHO-PHYSICAL TRANSFORMATIONS, SHOWN TO YOU AS A PARTING GIFT...
AT SOME POINT I FORESEE GREAT DANGER FOR YOU. THEN IT WILL BE THE TIME TO OPEN THIS SCROLL. DO NOT LOOK AT IT BEFORE.
NOW YOU ARE READY TO LEAVE. GO AND STAY IN THE SOLITUDE OF THE SNOW MOUNTAINS AND FORESTS. DEVOTE YOURSELF TO MEDITATION, AND I WILL NEVER FORGET YOU.
THE NEXT MORNING A PARTY CAME TO SEE ME OFF...
AND FOR HALF A DAY WE TRAVELED TOGETHER.
DAGMEMA OFFERED ME A PAIR OF BOOTS, PROVISIONS, AND A SKULL-CUP FILLED WITH NECTAR.
MY PATIENT AND ENERGETIC SON, DO NOT FORGET YOUR SPIRITUAL PARENTS. MAY
YOU HAVE STRENGTH AND PERSEVERANCE, AND MAY WE IN THE FUTURE MEET IN THE PURE BUDDHA-FIELDS.

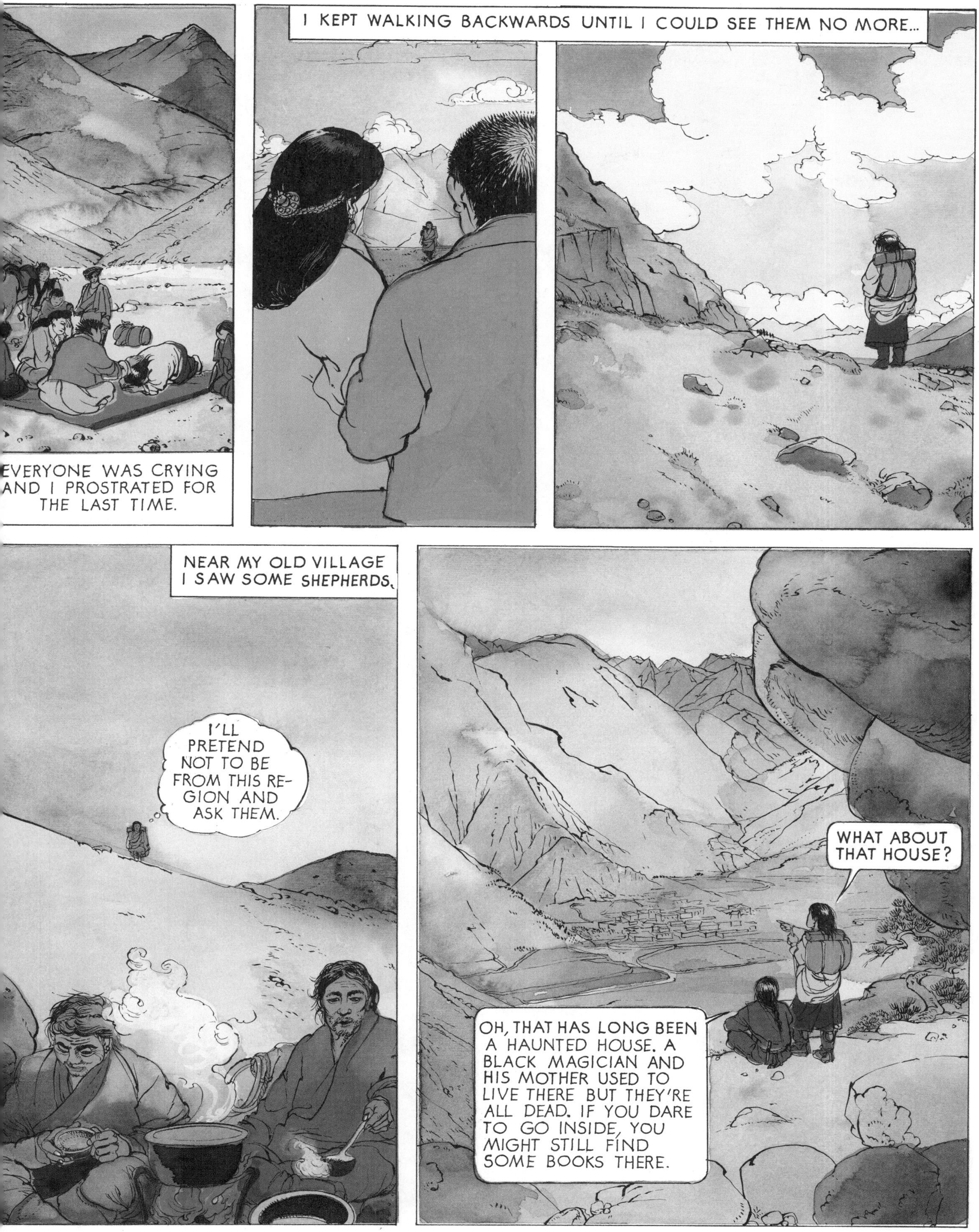
EVERYONE WAS CRYING AND I PROSTRATED FOR THE LAST TIME.
I KEPT WALKING BACKWARDS UNTIL I COULD SEE THEM NO MORE...
NEAR MY OLD VILLAGE I SAW SOME SHEPHERDS.
I'LL PRETEND NOT TO BE FROM THIS REGION AND ASK THEM.
WHAT ABOUT THAT HOUSE?
OH, THAT HAS LONG BEEN A HAUNTED HOUSE. A BLACK MAGICIAN AND HIS MOTHER USED TO LIVE THERE BUT THEY'RE ALL DEAD. IF YOU DARE TO GO INSIDE, YOU MIGHT STILL FIND SOME BOOKS THERE.

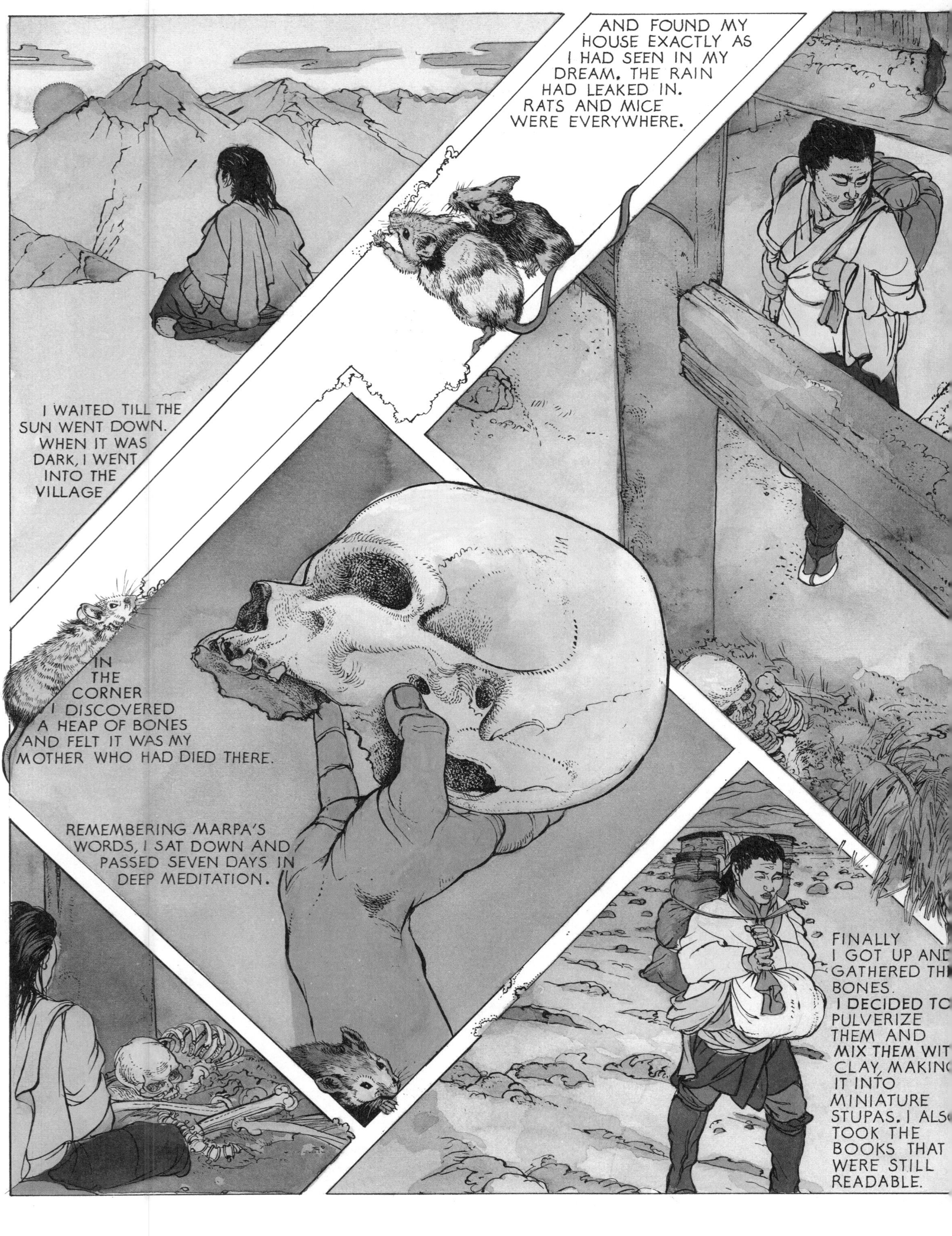
I WAITED TILL THE SUN WENT DOWN. WHEN IT WAS DARK, I WENT INTO THE VILLAGE
AND FOUND MY HOUSE EXACTLY AS I HAD SEEN IN MY DREAM. THE RAIN HAD LEAKED IN. RATS AND MICE WERE EVERYWHERE.
IN THE CORNER I DISCOVERED A HEAP OF BONES AND FELT IT WAS MY MOTHER WHO HAD DIED THERE.
REMEMBERING MARPA'S WORDS, I SAT DOWN AND PASSED SEVEN DAYS IN DEEP MEDITATION.
FINALLY I GOT UP AND GATHERED TH BONES. I DECIDED TO PULVERIZE THEM AND MIX THEM WIT CLAY, MAKING IT INTO MINIATURE STUPAS. I ALS TOOK THE BOOKS THAT WERE STILL READABLE.

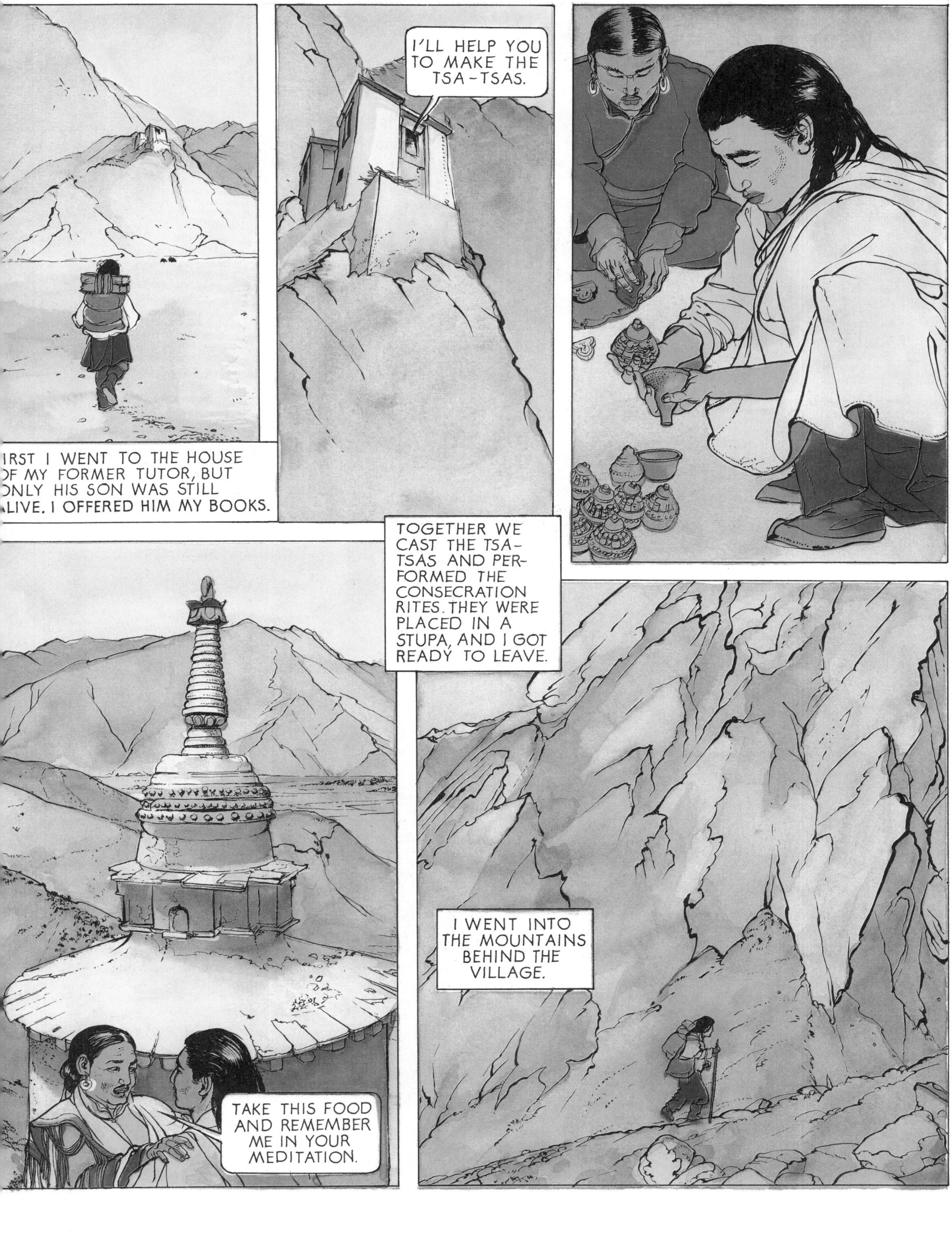
IRST I WENT TO THE HOUSE OF MY FORMER TUTOR, BUT ONLY HIS SON WAS STILL LIVE. I OFFERED HIM MY BOOKS.
I'LL HELP YOU TO MAKE THE TSA-TSAS.
TOGETHER WE CAST THE TSA-TSAS AND PERFORMED THE CONSECRATION RITES. THEY WERE PLACED IN A STUPA, AND I GOT READY TO LEAVE.
TAKE THIS FOOD AND REMEMBER ME IN YOUR MEDITATION.
I WENT INTO THE MOUNTAINS BEHIND THE VILLAGE.

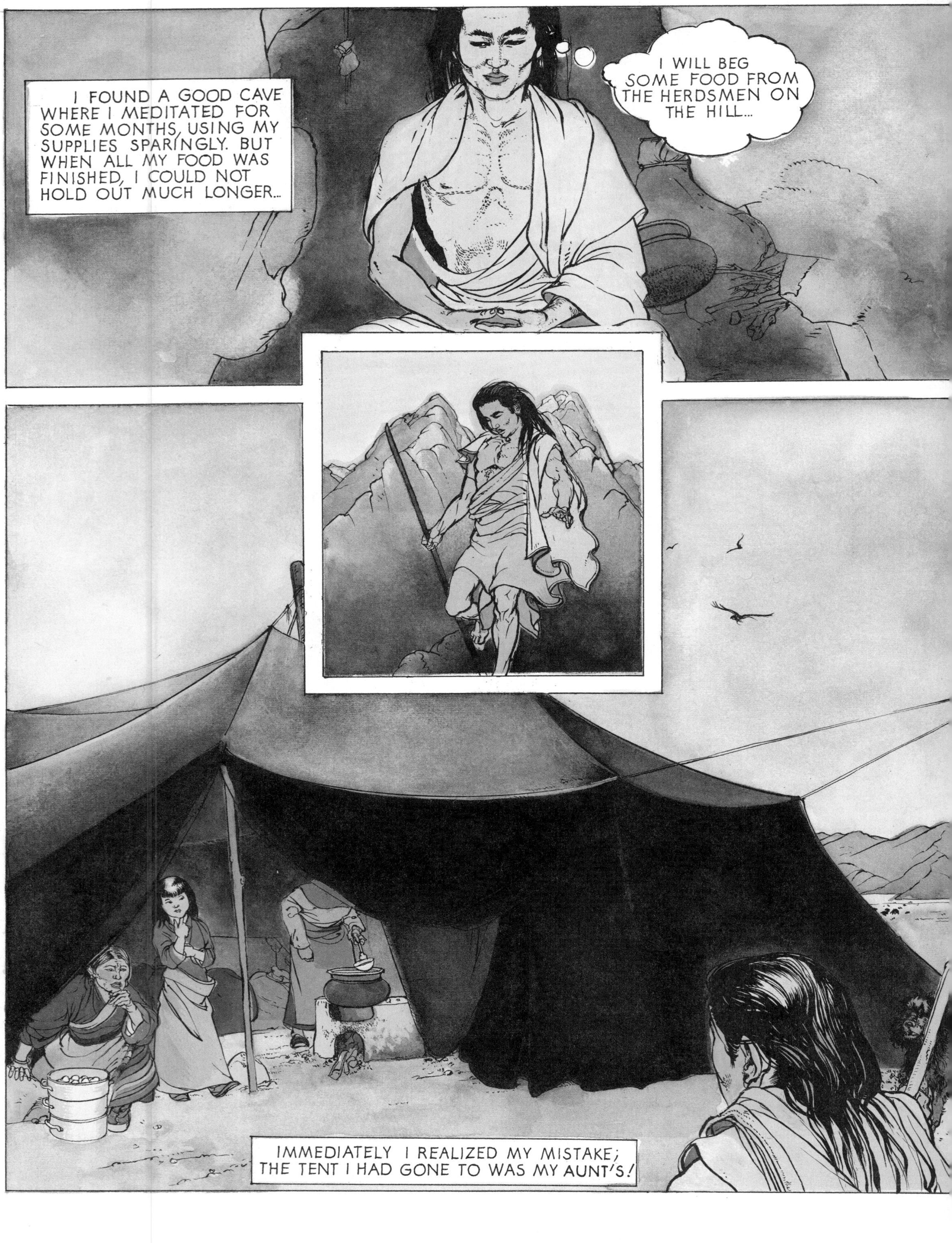
I FOUND A GOOD CAVE WHERE I MEDITATED FOR SOME MONTHS, USING MY SUPPLIES SPARINGLY. BUT WHEN ALL MY FOOD WAS FINISHED, I COULD NOT HOLD OUT MUCH LONGER...
I WILL BEG SOME FOOD FROM THE HERDSMEN ON THE HILL...
IMMEDIATELY I REALIZED MY MISTAKE; THE TENT I HAD GONE TO WAS MY AUNT'S!

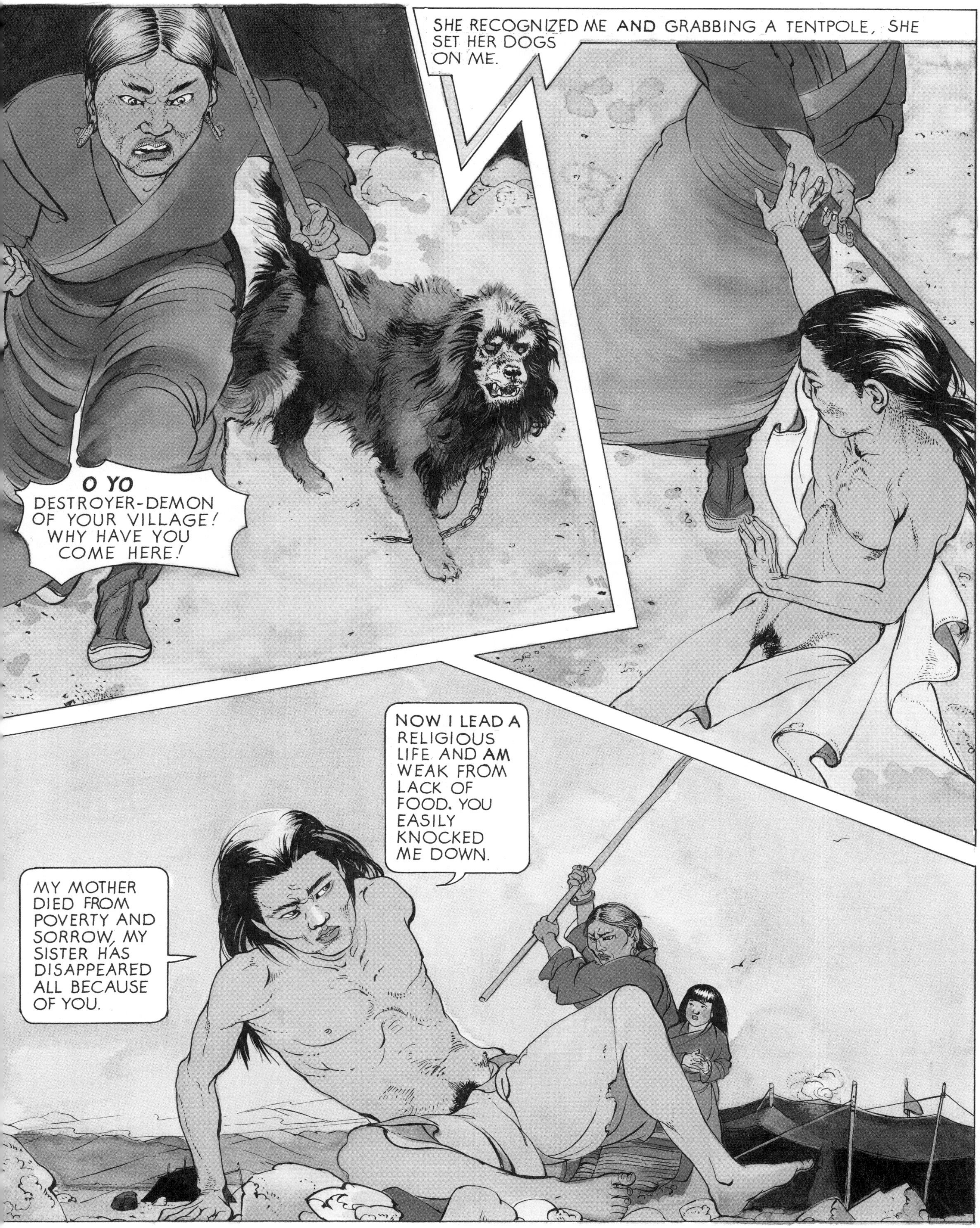
SHE RECOGNIZED ME AND GRABBING A TENTPOLE, SHE SET HER DOGS ON ME.
O YO DESTROYER-DEMON OF YOUR VILLAGE! WHY HAVE YOU COME HERE!
NOW I LEAD A RELIGIOUS LIFE AND AM WEAK FROM LACK OF FOOD. YOU EASILY KNOCKED ME DOWN.
MY MOTHER DIED FROM POVERTY AND SORROW, MY SISTER HAS DISAPPEARED ALL BECAUSE OF YOU.

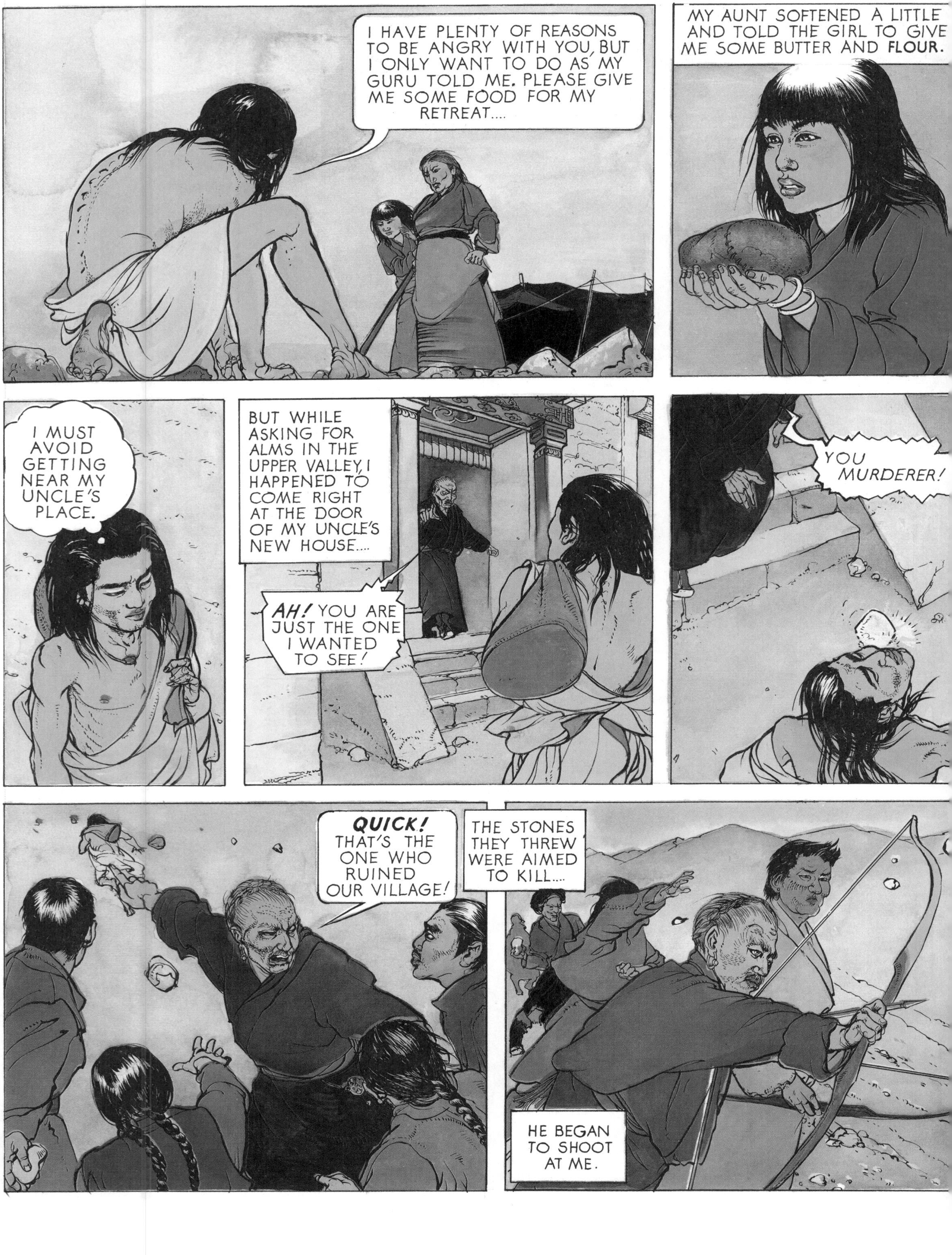
I HAVE PLENTY OF REASONS TO BE ANGRY WITH YOU, BUT I ONLY WANT TO DO AS MY GURU TOLD ME. PLEASE GIVE ME SOME FOOD FOR MY RETREAT....
MY AUNT SOFTENED A LITTLE AND TOLD THE GIRL TO GIVE ME SOME BUTTER AND FLOUR.
I MUST AVOID GETTING NEAR MY UNCLE'S PLACE.
BUT WHILE ASKING FOR ALMS IN THE UPPER VALLEY, I HAPPENED TO COME RIGHT AT THE DOOR OF MY UNCLE'S NEW HOUSE....
AH! YOU ARE JUST THE ONE I WANTED TO SEE!
YOU MURDERER!
QUICK! THAT'S THE ONE WHO RUINED OUR VILLAGE!
THE STONES THEY THREW WERE AIMED TO KILL....
HE BEGAN TO SHOOT AT ME.

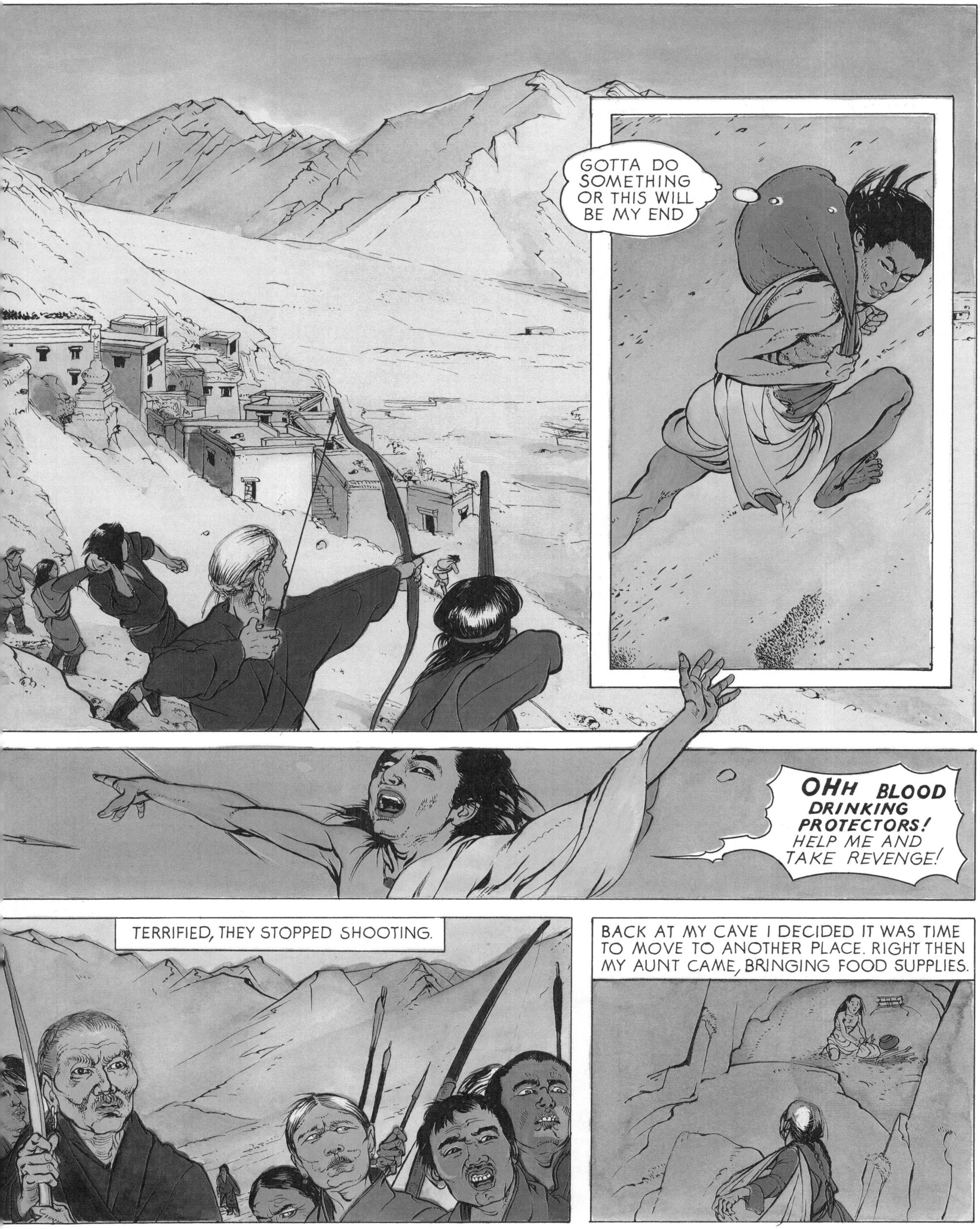
GOTTA DO SOMETHING OR THIS WILL BE MY END
OHH BLOOD DRINKING PROTECTORS! HELP ME AND TAKE REVENGE!
TERRIFIED, THEY STOPPED SHOOTING.
BACK AT MY CAVE I DECIDED IT WAS TIME TO MOVE TO ANOTHER PLACE. RIGHT THEN MY AUNT CAME, BRINGING FOOD SUPPLIES.

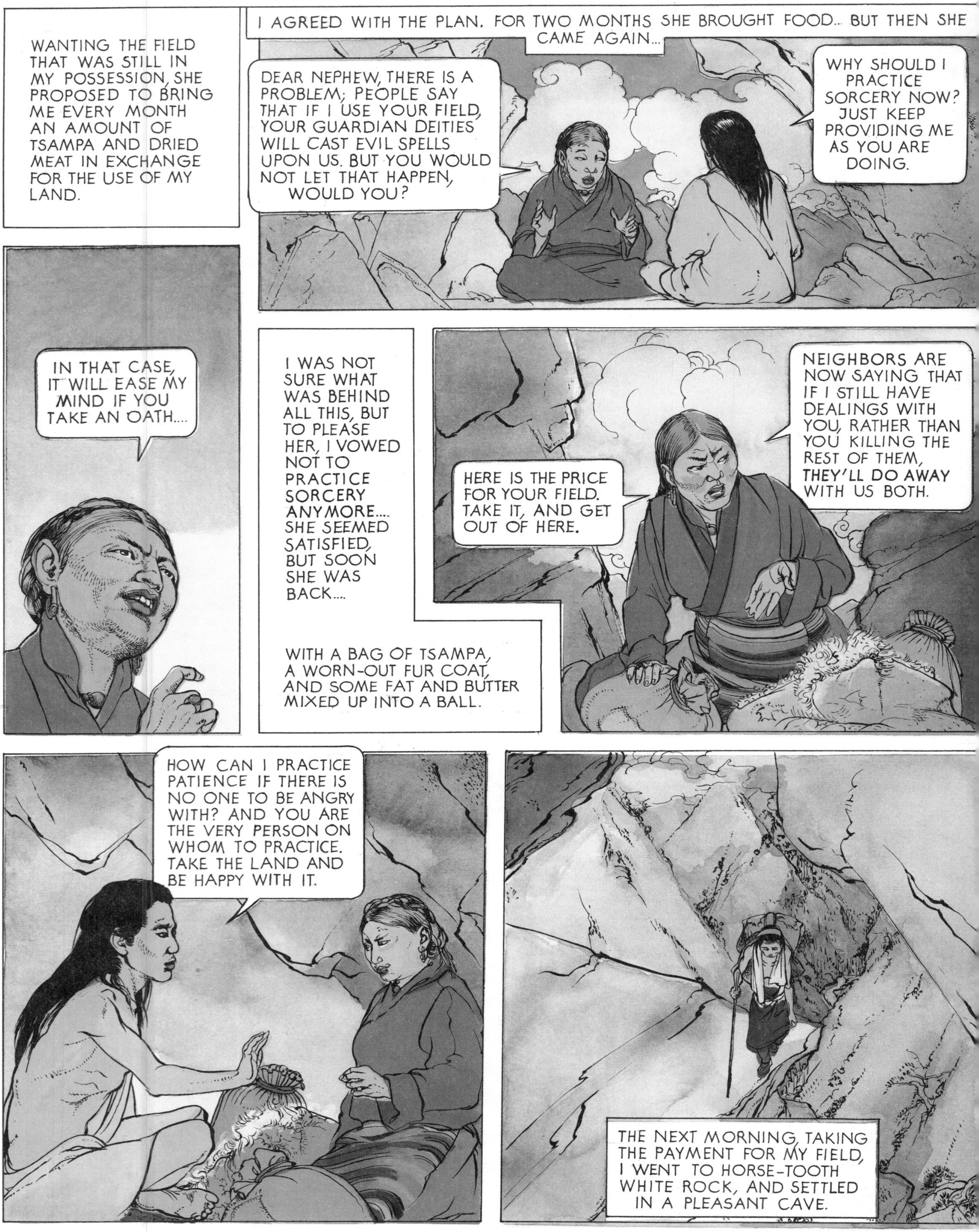
WANTING THE FIELD THAT WAS STILL IN MY POSSESSION, SHE PROPOSED TO BRING ME EVERY MONTH AN AMOUNT OF TSAMPA AND DRIED MEAT IN EXCHANGE FOR THE USE OF MY LAND.
I AGREED WITH THE PLAN. FOR TWO MONTHS SHE BROUGHT FOOD... BUT THEN SHE CAME AGAIN...
DEAR NEPHEW, THERE IS A PROBLEM; PEOPLE SAY THAT IF I USE YOUR FIELD, YOUR GUARDIAN DEITIES WILL CAST EVIL SPELLS UPON US. BUT YOU WOULD NOT LET THAT HAPPEN, WOULD YOU?
WHY SHOULD I PRACTICE SORCERY NOW? JUST KEEP PROVIDING ME AS YOU ARE DOING.
IN THAT CASE, IT WILL EASE MY MIND IF YOU TAKE AN OATH....
I WAS NOT SURE WHAT WAS BEHIND ALL THIS, BUT TO PLEASE HER, I VOWED NOT TO PRACTICE SORCERY ANYMORE.... SHE SEEMED SATISFIED, BUT SOON SHE WAS BACK....
WITH A BAG OF TSAMPA, A WORN-OUT FUR COAT, AND SOME FAT AND BUTTER MIXED UP INTO A BALL.
NEIGHBORS ARE NOW SAYING THAT IF I STILL HAVE DEALINGS WITH YOU, RATHER THAN YOU KILLING THE REST OF THEM, **THEY'LL DO AWAY** WITH US BOTH.
HERE IS THE PRICE FOR YOUR FIELD. TAKE IT, AND GET OUT OF HERE.
HOW CAN I PRACTICE PATIENCE IF THERE IS NO ONE TO BE ANGRY WITH? AND YOU ARE THE VERY PERSON ON WHOM TO PRACTICE. TAKE THE LAND AND BE HAPPY WITH IT.
THE NEXT MORNING, TAKING THE PAYMENT FOR MY FIELD, I WENT TO HORSE-TOOTH WHITE ROCK, AND SETTLED IN A PLEASANT CAVE.

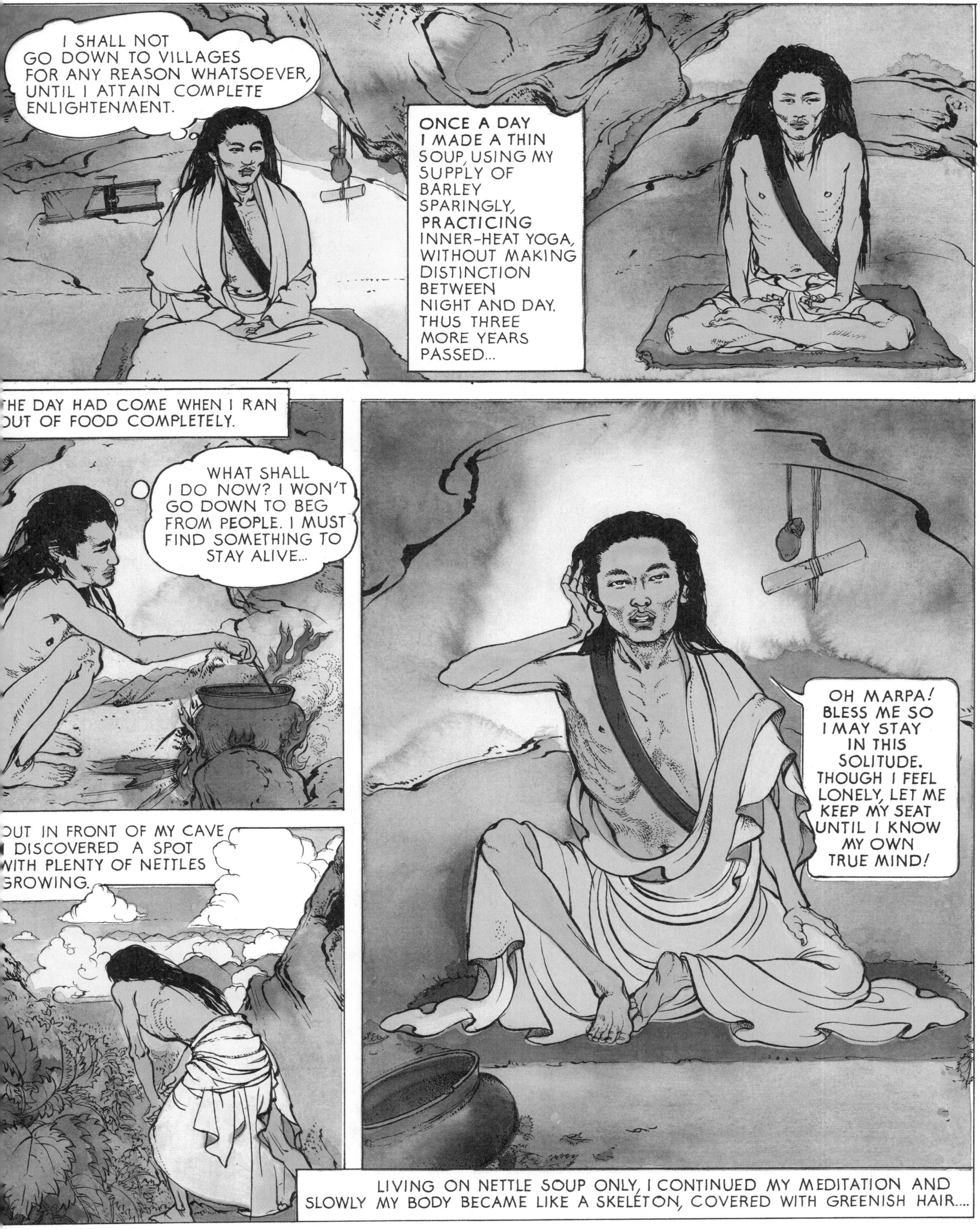

I SHALL NOT GO DOWN TO VILLAGES FOR ANY REASON WHATSOEVER, UNTIL I ATTAIN COMPLETE ENLIGHTENMENT.
ONCE A DAY I MADE A THIN SOUP, USING MY SUPPLY OF BARLEY SPARINGLY, PRACTICING INNER-HEAT YOGA, WITHOUT MAKING DISTINCTION BETWEEN NIGHT AND DAY. THUS THREE MORE YEARS PASSED...
THE DAY HAD COME WHEN I RAN OUT OF FOOD COMPLETELY.
WHAT SHALL I DO NOW? I WON'T GO DOWN TO BEG FROM PEOPLE. I MUST FIND SOMETHING TO STAY ALIVE...
OUT IN FRONT OF MY CAVE I DISCOVERED A SPOT WITH PLENTY OF NETTLES GROWING.
OH MARPA! BLESS ME SO I MAY STAY IN THIS SOLITUDE. THOUGH I FEEL LONELY, LET ME KEEP MY SEAT UNTIL I KNOW MY OWN TRUE MIND!
LIVING ON NETTLE SOUP ONLY, I CONTINUED MY MEDITATION AND SLOWLY MY BODY BECAME LIKE A SKELETON, COVERED WITH GREENISH HAIR....

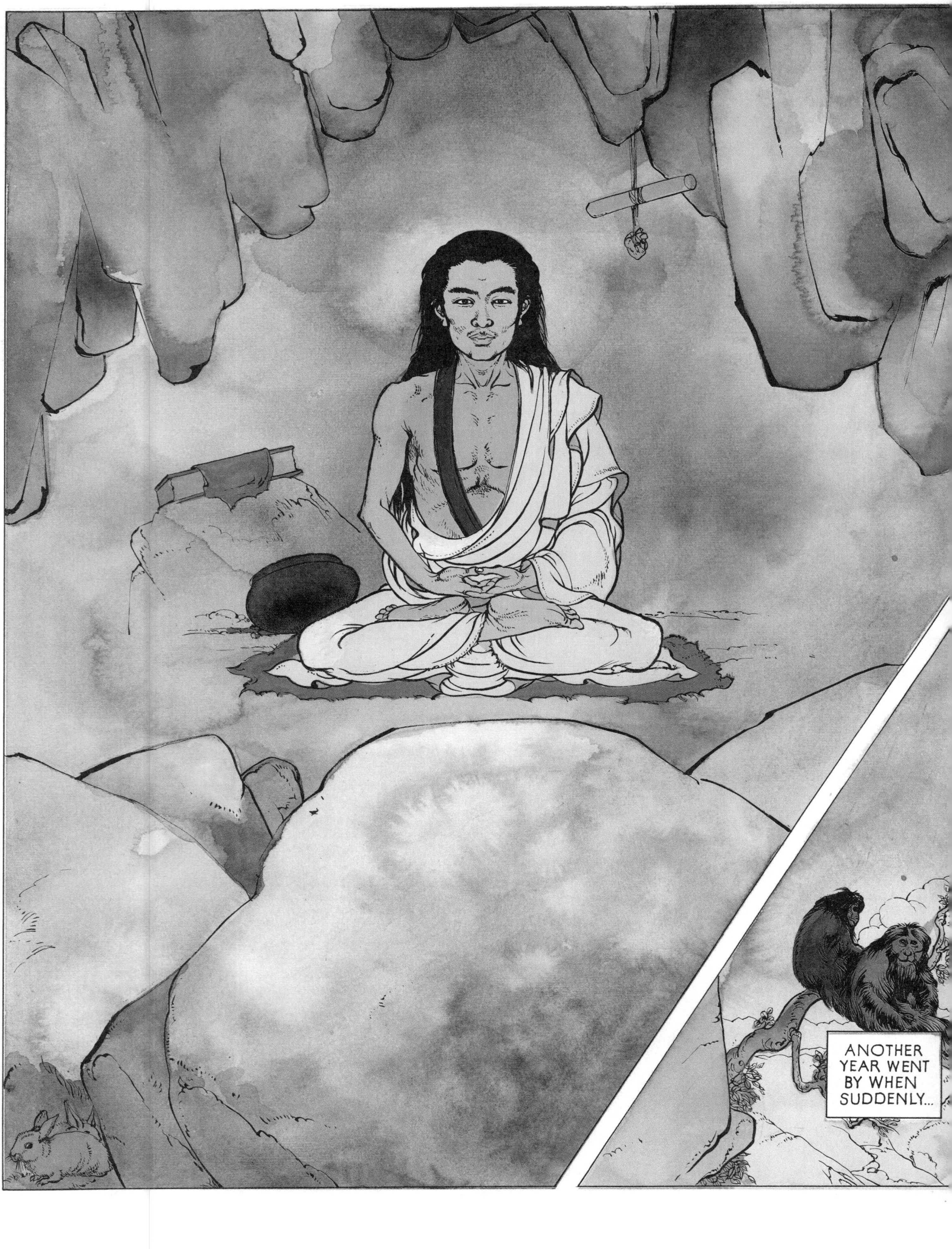
ANOTHER YEAR WENT BY WHEN SUDDENLY...

A GROUP OF HUNTERS WHO HAD NOT CAUGHT ANYTHING PASSED BY MY CAVE...

LOOK! A GHOST!

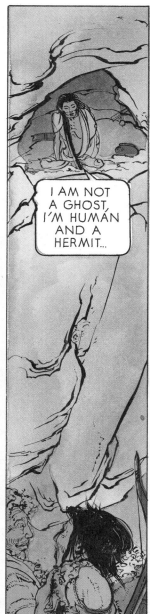

I AM NOT A GHOST, I'M HUMAN AND A HERMIT...

WHERE IS YOUR FOOD? YOU SHOULD GIVE US SOME, OR ELSE....

I HAVE NOTHING BUT NETTLES.

LET'S BOUNCE HIM A LITTLE!

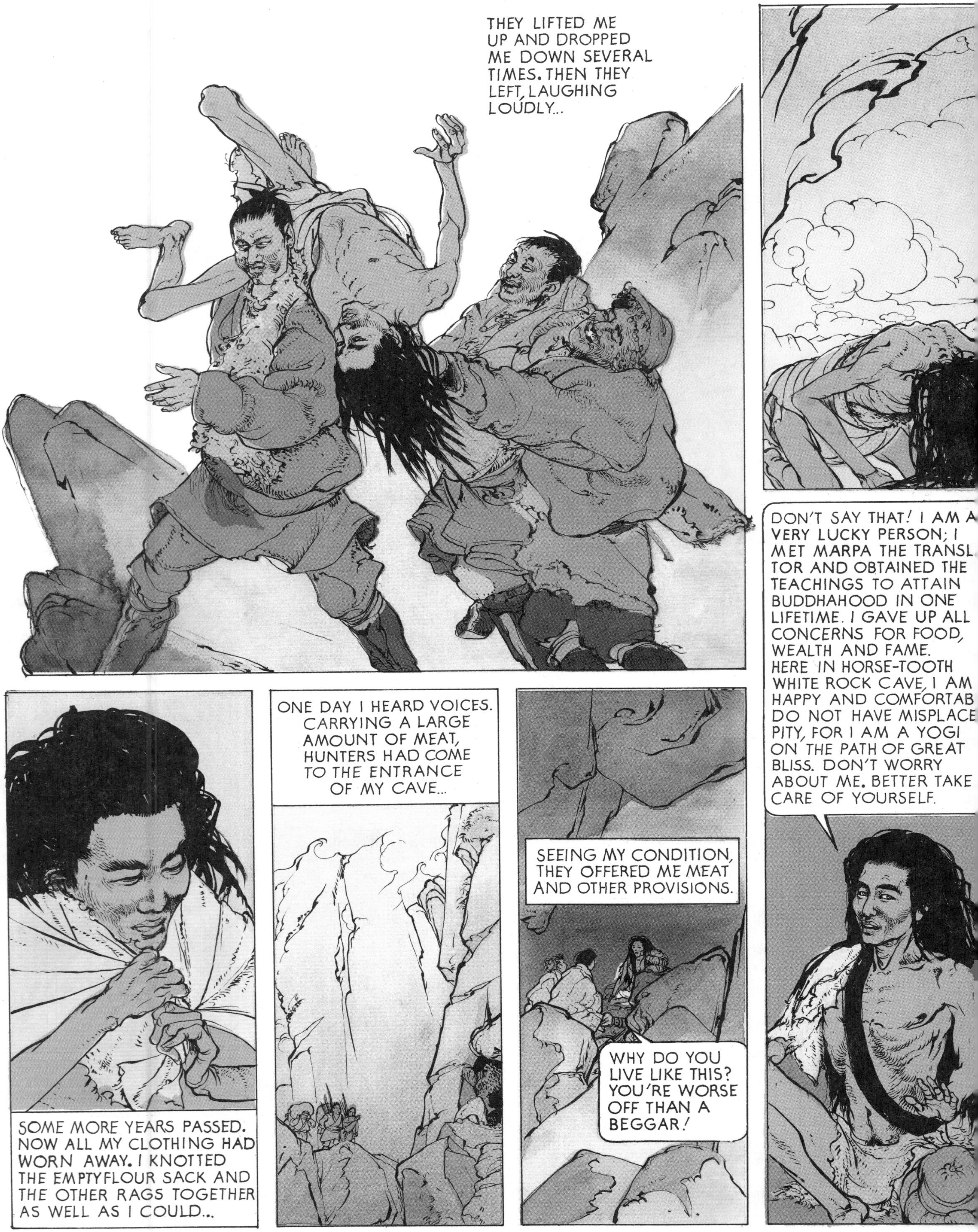

THEY LIFTED ME UP AND DROPPED ME DOWN SEVERAL TIMES. THEN THEY LEFT, LAUGHING LOUDLY...
SOME MORE YEARS PASSED. NOW ALL MY CLOTHING HAD WORN AWAY. I KNOTTED THE EMPTYFLOUR SACK AND THE OTHER RAGS TOGETHER AS WELL AS I COULD...
ONE DAY I HEARD VOICES. CARRYING A LARGE AMOUNT OF MEAT, HUNTERS HAD COME TO THE ENTRANCE OF MY CAVE...
SEEING MY CONDITION, THEY OFFERED ME MEAT AND OTHER PROVISIONS.
WHY DO YOU LIVE LIKE THIS? YOU'RE WORSE OFF THAN A BEGGAR!
DON'T SAY THAT! I AM A VERY LUCKY PERSON; I MET MARPA THE TRANSL TOR AND OBTAINED THE TEACHINGS TO ATTAIN BUDDHAHOOD IN ONE LIFETIME. I GAVE UP ALL CONCERNS FOR FOOD, WEALTH AND FAME. HERE IN HORSE-TOOTH WHITE ROCK CAVE, I AM HAPPY AND COMFORTAB DO NOT HAVE MISPLACE PITY, FOR I AM A YOGI ON THE PATH OF GREAT BLISS. DON'T WORRY ABOUT ME. BETTER TAKE CARE OF YOURSELF.

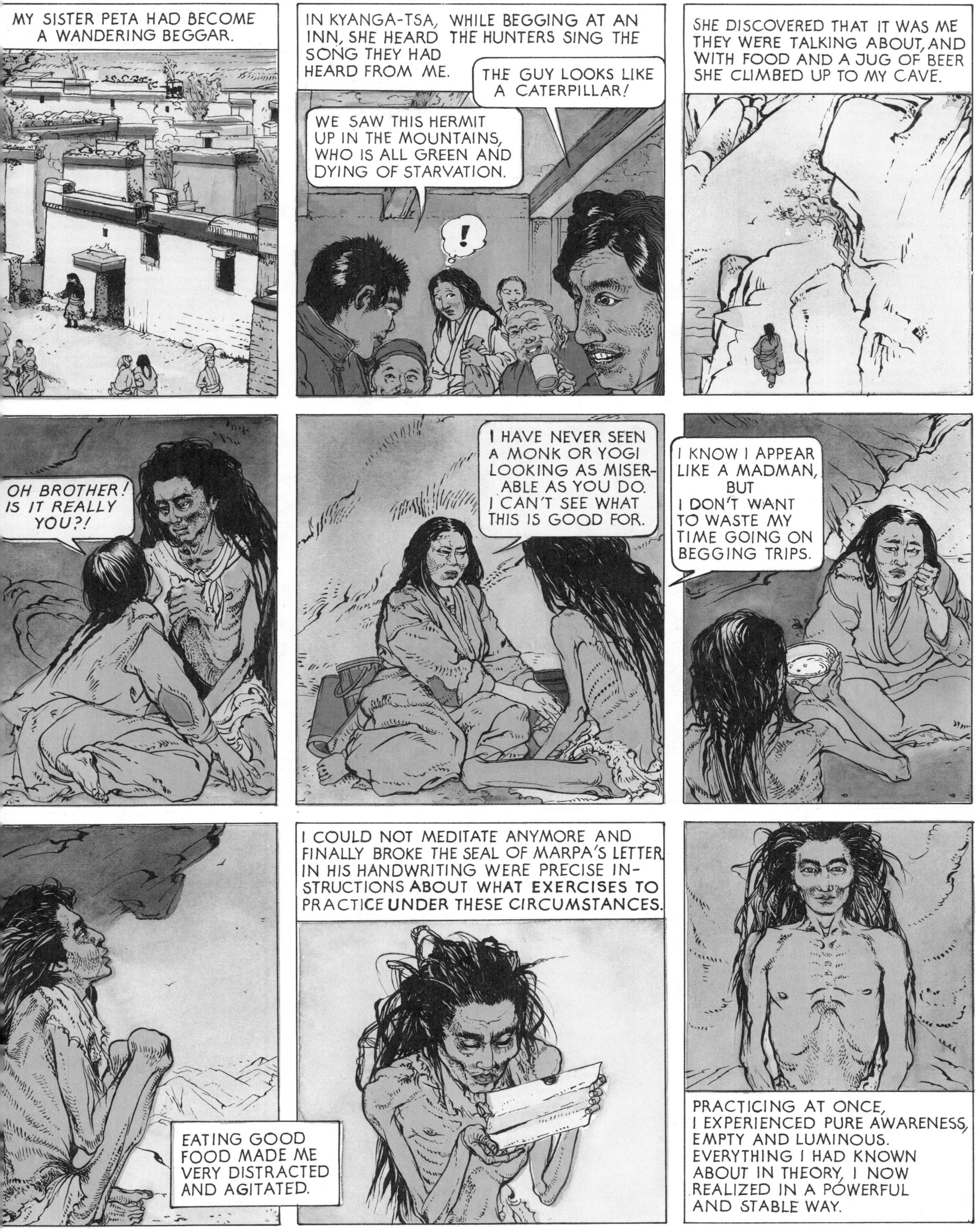
MY SISTER PETA HAD BECOME A WANDERING BEGGAR.
IN KYANGA-TSA, WHILE BEGGING AT AN INN, SHE HEARD THE HUNTERS SING THE SONG THEY HAD HEARD FROM ME.
THE GUY LOOKS LIKE A CATERPILLAR!
WE SAW THIS HERMIT UP IN THE MOUNTAINS, WHO IS ALL GREEN AND DYING OF STARVATION.
!
SHE DISCOVERED THAT IT WAS ME THEY WERE TALKING ABOUT, AND WITH FOOD AND A JUG OF BEER SHE CLIMBED UP TO MY CAVE.
OH BROTHER! IS IT REALLY YOU?!
I HAVE NEVER SEEN A MONK OR YOGI LOOKING AS MISER-ABLE AS YOU DO. I CAN'T SEE WHAT THIS IS GOOD FOR.
I KNOW I APPEAR LIKE A MADMAN, BUT I DON'T WANT TO WASTE MY TIME GOING ON BEGGING TRIPS.
EATING GOOD FOOD MADE ME VERY DISTRACTED AND AGITATED.
I COULD NOT MEDITATE ANYMORE AND FINALLY BROKE THE SEAL OF MARPA'S LETTER. IN HIS HANDWRITING WERE PRECISE IN-STRUCTIONS ABOUT WHAT EXERCISES TO PRACTICE UNDER THESE CIRCUMSTANCES.
PRACTICING AT ONCE, I EXPERIENCED PURE AWARENESS, EMPTY AND LUMINOUS. EVERYTHING I HAD KNOWN ABOUT IN THEORY, I NOW REALIZED IN A POWERFUL AND STABLE WAY.

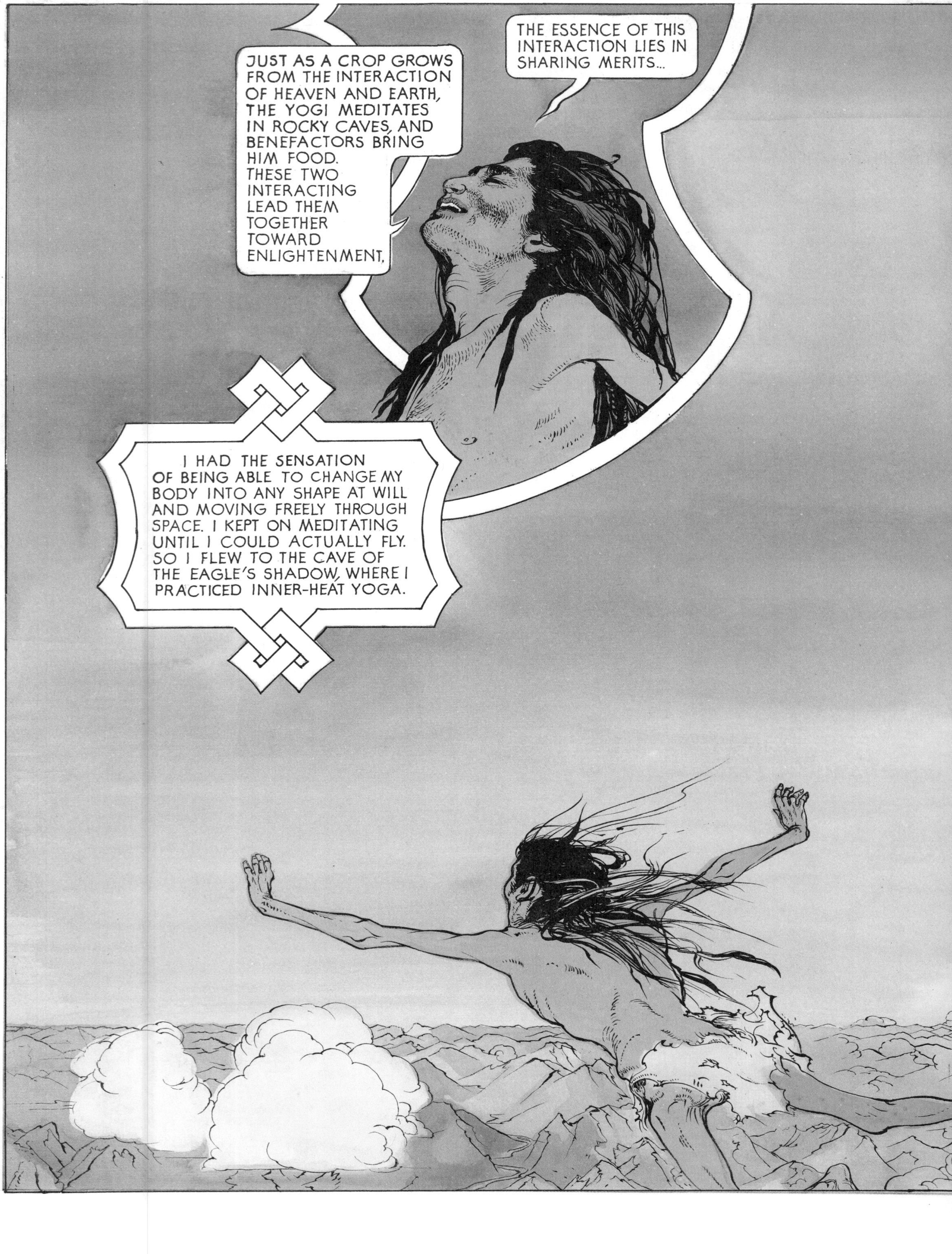
JUST AS A CROP GROWS FROM THE INTERACTION OF HEAVEN AND EARTH, THE YOGI MEDITATES IN ROCKY CAVES, AND BENEFACTORS BRING HIM FOOD. THESE TWO INTERACTING LEAD THEM TOGETHER TOWARD ENLIGHTENMENT,
THE ESSENCE OF THIS INTERACTION LIES IN SHARING MERITS...
I HAD THE SENSATION OF BEING ABLE TO CHANGE MY BODY INTO ANY SHAPE AT WILL AND MOVING FREELY THROUGH SPACE. I KEPT ON MEDITATING UNTIL I COULD ACTUALLY FLY. SO I FLEW TO THE CAVE OF THE EAGLE'S SHADOW, WHERE I PRACTICED INNER-HEAT YOGA.

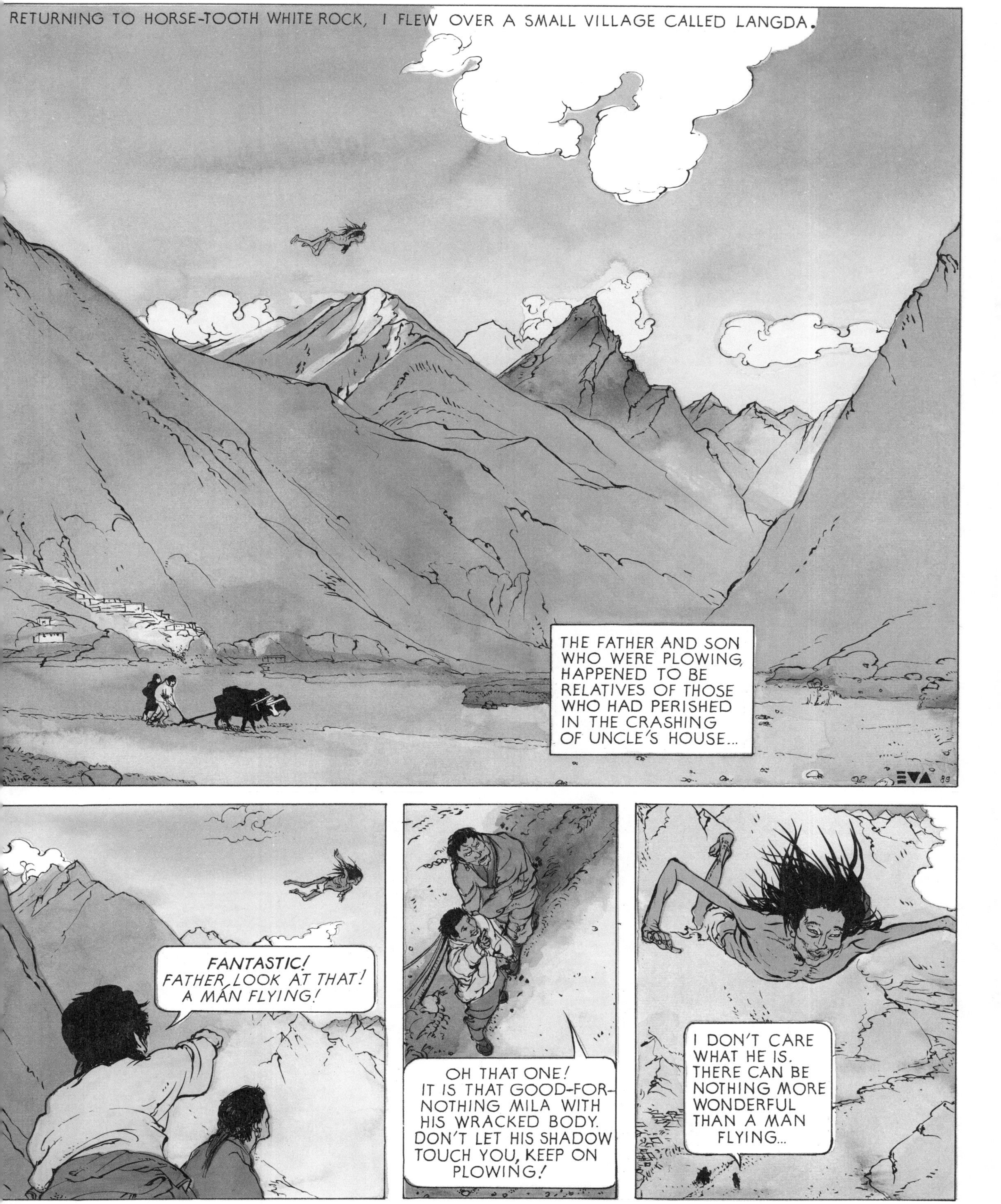
RETURNING TO HORSE-TOOTH WHITE ROCK, I FLEW OVER A SMALL VILLAGE CALLED LANGDA.
THE FATHER AND SON WHO WERE PLOWING, HAPPENED TO BE RELATIVES OF THOSE WHO HAD PERISHED IN THE CRASHING OF UNCLE'S HOUSE...
FANTASTIC! FATHER, LOOK AT THAT! A MAN FLYING!
OH THAT ONE! IT IS THAT GOOD-FOR-NOTHING MILA WITH HIS WRACKED BODY. DON'T LET HIS SHADOW TOUCH YOU, KEEP ON PLOWING!
I DON'T CARE WHAT HE IS. THERE CAN BE NOTHING MORE WONDERFUL THAN A MAN FLYING...

SOON THE NEWS SPREAD THAT I HAD BEEN SEEN FLYING.

IF I STAY HERE ANY LONGER, MORE AND MORE PEOPLE WILL COME TO SEE ME TO ASK FOR MAGIC SPELLS AND PROTECTIONS. IT MIGHT DISTURB MY MEDITATION. I WILL GO TO CHUBAR.

* NEAR MOUNT EVEREST

ON MY WAY, NEAR THE VILLAGE OF TINGRI, I WAS LYING BY THE ROAD, ENJOYING THE VIEW, WHEN SOME PRETTY GIRLS, ALL DRESSED UP, PASSED ME.

WHAT A DEPRESSING SIGHT...

LOOK WHAT A MISERABLE MAN!

IT REALLY UPSETS ME TO SEE THIS.

GIRLS, YOU ARE SO PROUD, YOU GOT IT ALL WRONG. LISTEN TO MY SONG: IN THESE DARK DAYS OF THE KALI-YUGA, EVIL PEOPLE ARE POPULAR AND STARS, THE GOOD ONES, **ARE IGNORED.**

IN THE EYES OF THE BEAUTIFUL GIRL THE HANDSOME MAN IS PREFERRED, THE HERMIT IS IGNORED. YOU GIRLS, ALL DRESSED UP, WHO THINK MARRIAGE IS THE MOST DESIRABLE OF ALL THINGS AND I, MILAREPA, HAVE MUTUAL CONTEMPT AND PITY.

IT'S THE FAMOUS MILAREPA!

WE SAID SOME REALLY STUPID THINGS!

PLEASE, SING SOME MORE.

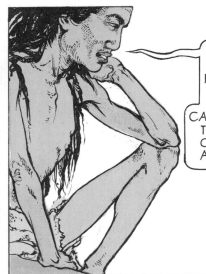

SOME CARE ONLY FOR SCIENCE, SOME ONLY FOR WEALTH. SOME CARE FOR GLAMOUR, AND GENERALLY NOBODY CARES FOR THE PROFOUND TRUTH, JUST AS YOU GIRLS CARE FOR LOVE-SONGS AND THE DHARMA SOUNDS BORING TO YOU.

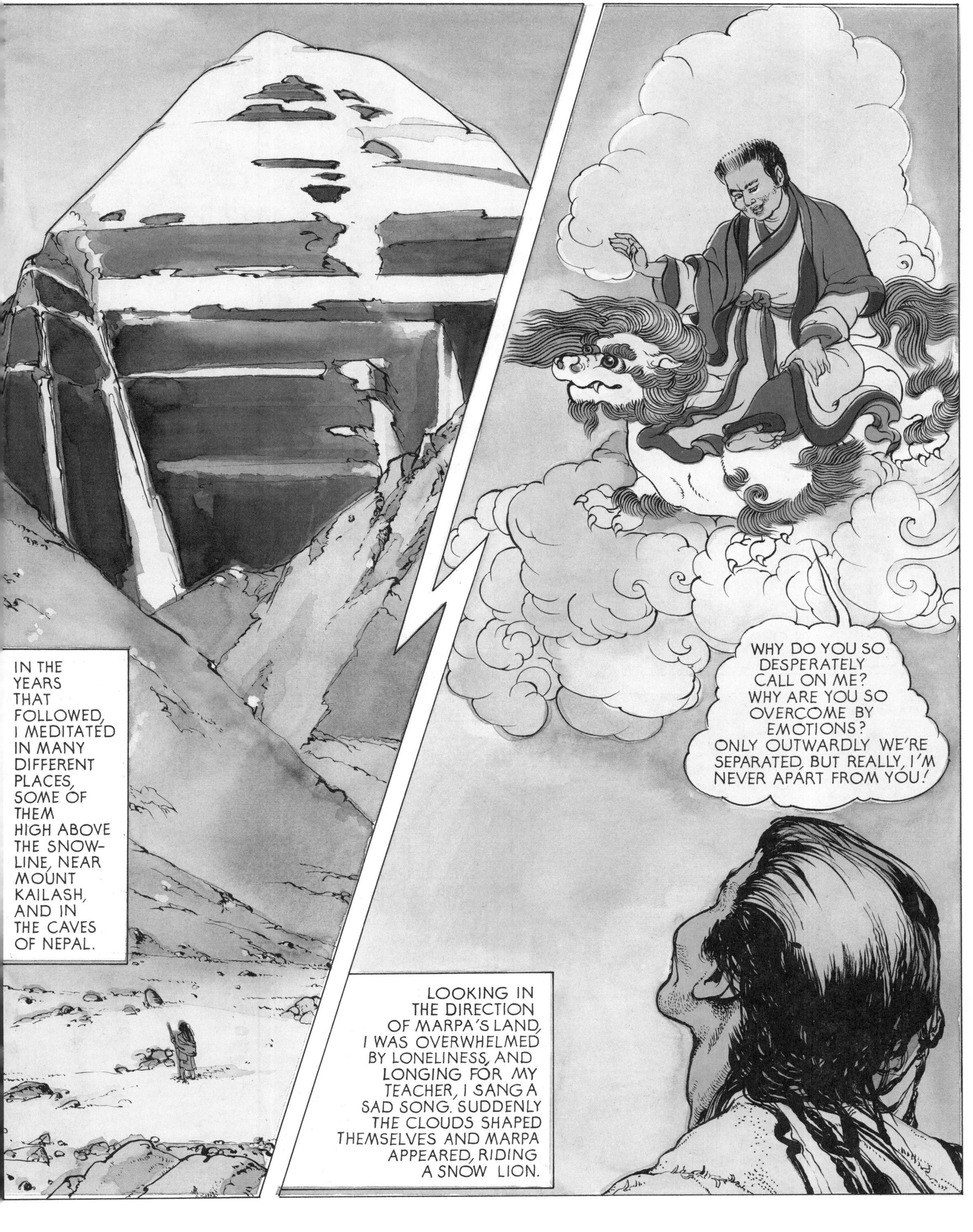
IN THE YEARS THAT FOLLOWED, I MEDITATED IN MANY DIFFERENT PLACES, SOME OF THEM HIGH ABOVE THE SNOW-LINE, NEAR MOUNT KAILASH, AND IN THE CAVES OF NEPAL.
LOOKING IN THE DIRECTION OF MARPA'S LAND, I WAS OVERWHELMED BY LONELINESS, AND LONGING FOR MY TEACHER, I SANG A SAD SONG. SUDDENLY THE CLOUDS SHAPED THEMSELVES AND MARPA APPEARED, RIDING A SNOW LION.
WHY DO YOU SO DESPERATELY CALL ON ME? WHY ARE YOU SO OVERCOME BY EMOTIONS? ONLY OUTWARDLY WE'RE SEPARATED, BUT REALLY, I'M NEVER APART FROM YOU!

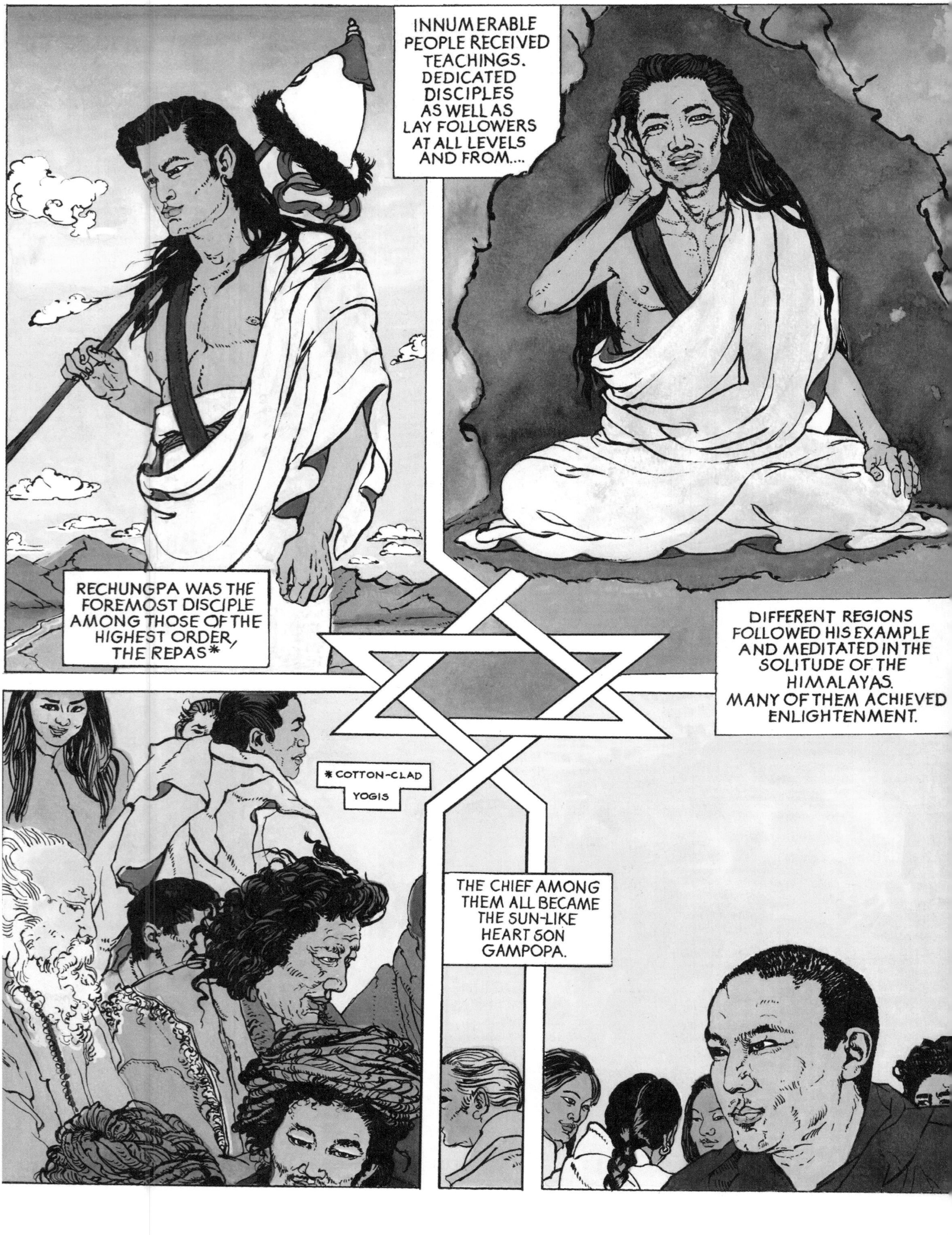
INNUMERABLE PEOPLE RECEIVED TEACHINGS. DEDICATED DISCIPLES AS WELL AS LAY FOLLOWERS AT ALL LEVELS AND FROM....
RECHUNGPA WAS THE FOREMOST DISCIPLE AMONG THOSE OF THE HIGHEST ORDER, THE REPAS*
DIFFERENT REGIONS FOLLOWED HIS EXAMPLE AND MEDITATED IN THE SOLITUDE OF THE HIMALAYAS. MANY OF THEM ACHIEVED ENLIGHTENMENT.
* COTTON-CLAD YOGIS
THE CHIEF AMONG THEM ALL BECAME THE SUN-LIKE HEART SON GAMPOPA.

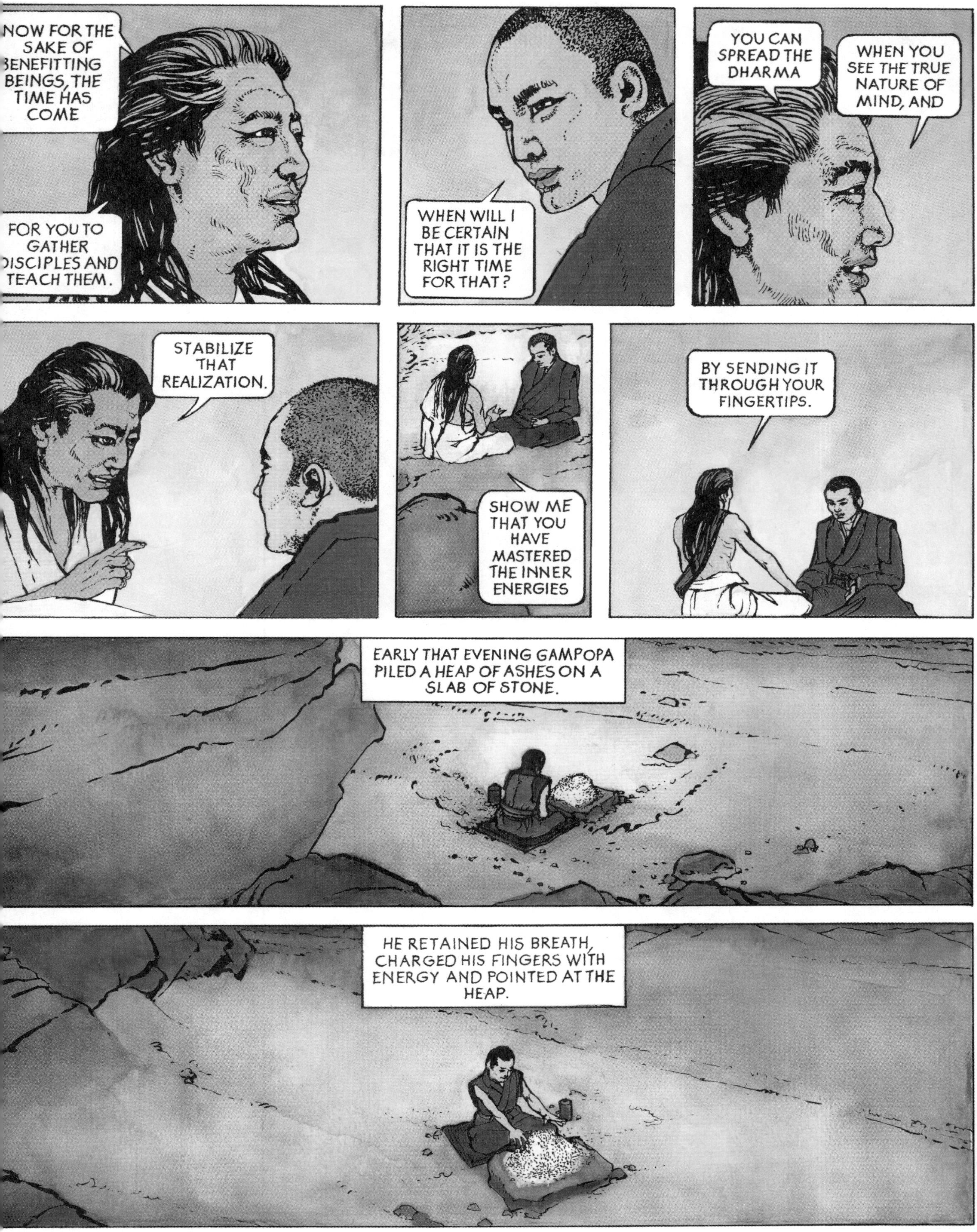
NOW FOR THE SAKE OF BENEFITTING BEINGS, THE TIME HAS COME
FOR YOU TO GATHER DISCIPLES AND TEACH THEM.
WHEN WILL I BE CERTAIN THAT IT IS THE RIGHT TIME FOR THAT?
WHEN YOU SEE THE TRUE NATURE OF MIND, AND
YOU CAN SPREAD THE DHARMA
STABILIZE THAT REALIZATION.
SHOW ME THAT YOU HAVE MASTERED THE INNER ENERGIES
BY SENDING IT THROUGH YOUR FINGERTIPS.
EARLY THAT EVENING GAMPOPA PILED A HEAP OF ASHES ON A SLAB OF STONE.
HE RETAINED HIS BREATH, CHARGED HIS FINGERS WITH ENERGY AND POINTED AT THE HEAP.

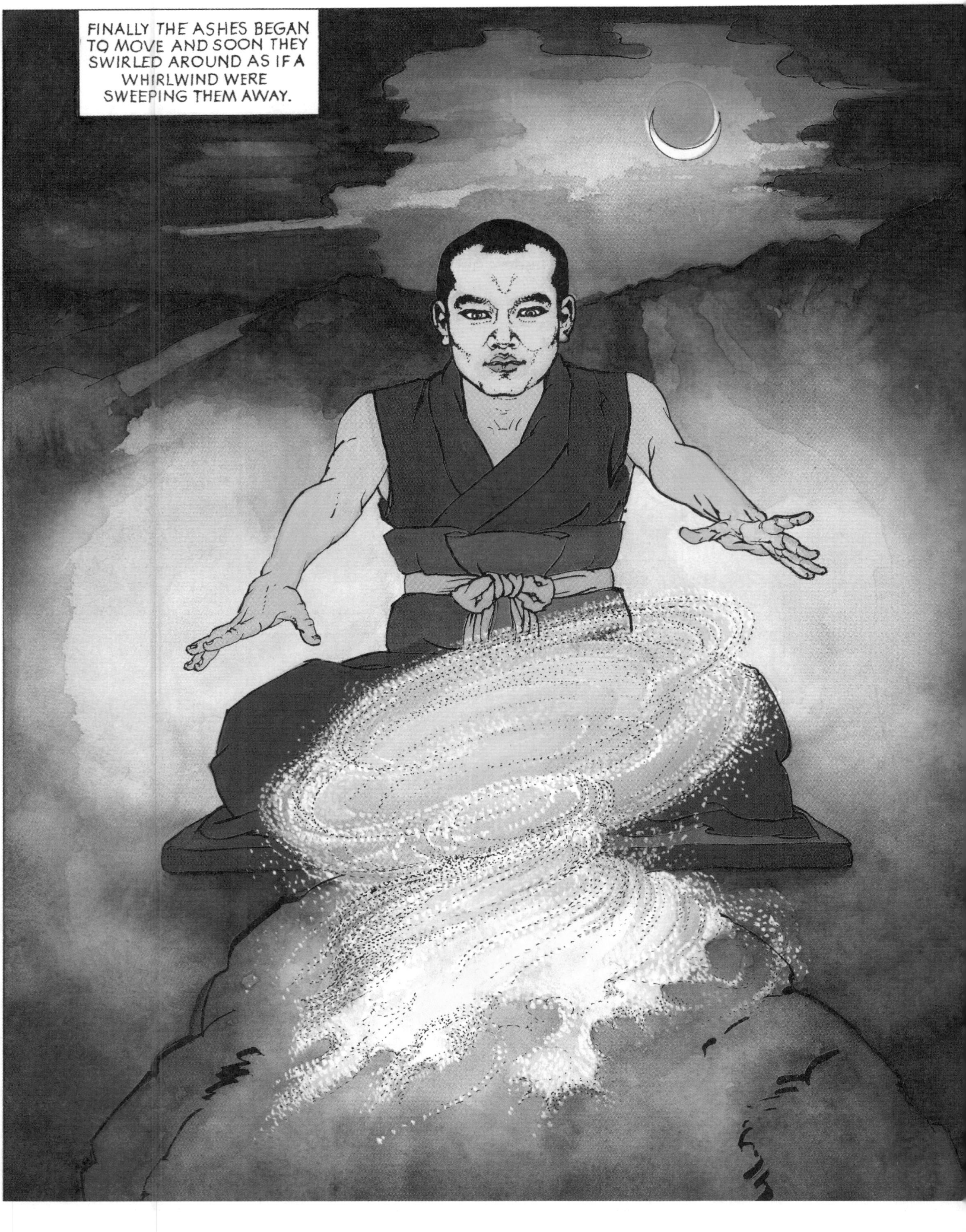
FINALLY THE ASHES BEGAN TO MOVE AND SOON THEY SWIRLED AROUND AS IF A WHIRLWIND WERE SWEEPING THEM AWAY.

NOW RETURN TO YOUR HOMELAND OF CENTRAL TIBET

AND MEDITATE THERE!

I WILL SEE YOU OFF

AND ESCORT YOU FOR A WHILE.

GAMPOPA WENT TO SAY GOODBYE TO HIS FELLOW DISCIPLES AND IT WAS CLEAR THAT HE WOULD BE SORELY MISSED.

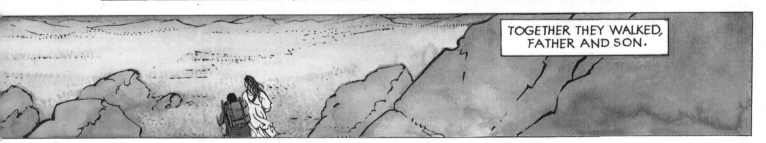

TOGETHER THEY WALKED, FATHER AND SON.

THERE ARE A FEW MORE TEACHINGS I WISH TO GIVE YOU.

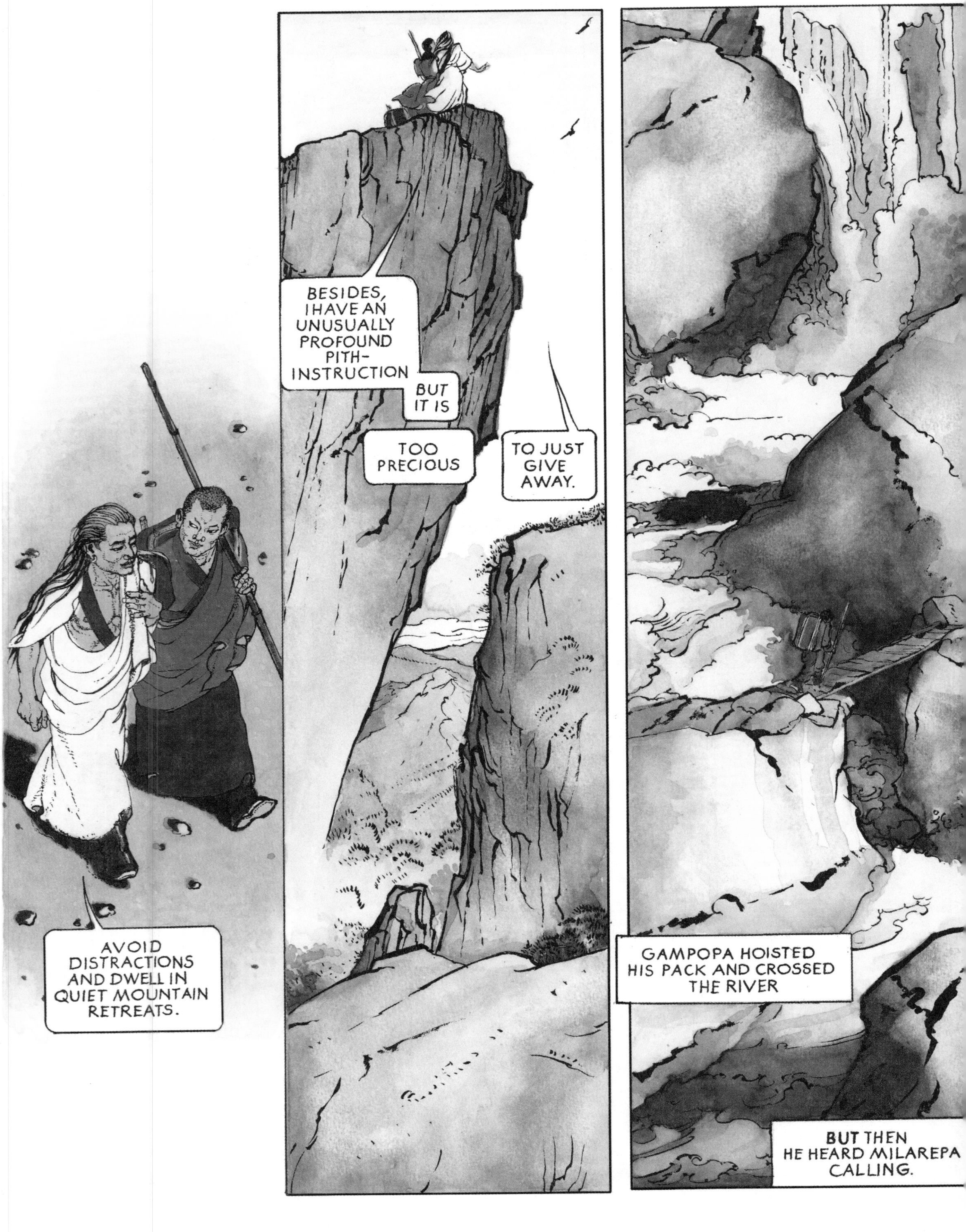
AVOID DISTRACTIONS AND DWELL IN QUIET MOUNTAIN RETREATS.
BESIDES, I HAVE AN UNUSUALLY PROFOUND PITH-INSTRUCTION
BUT IT IS
TOO PRECIOUS
TO JUST GIVE AWAY.
GAMPOPA HOISTED HIS PACK AND CROSSED THE RIVER
BUT THEN HE HEARD MILAREPA CALLING.

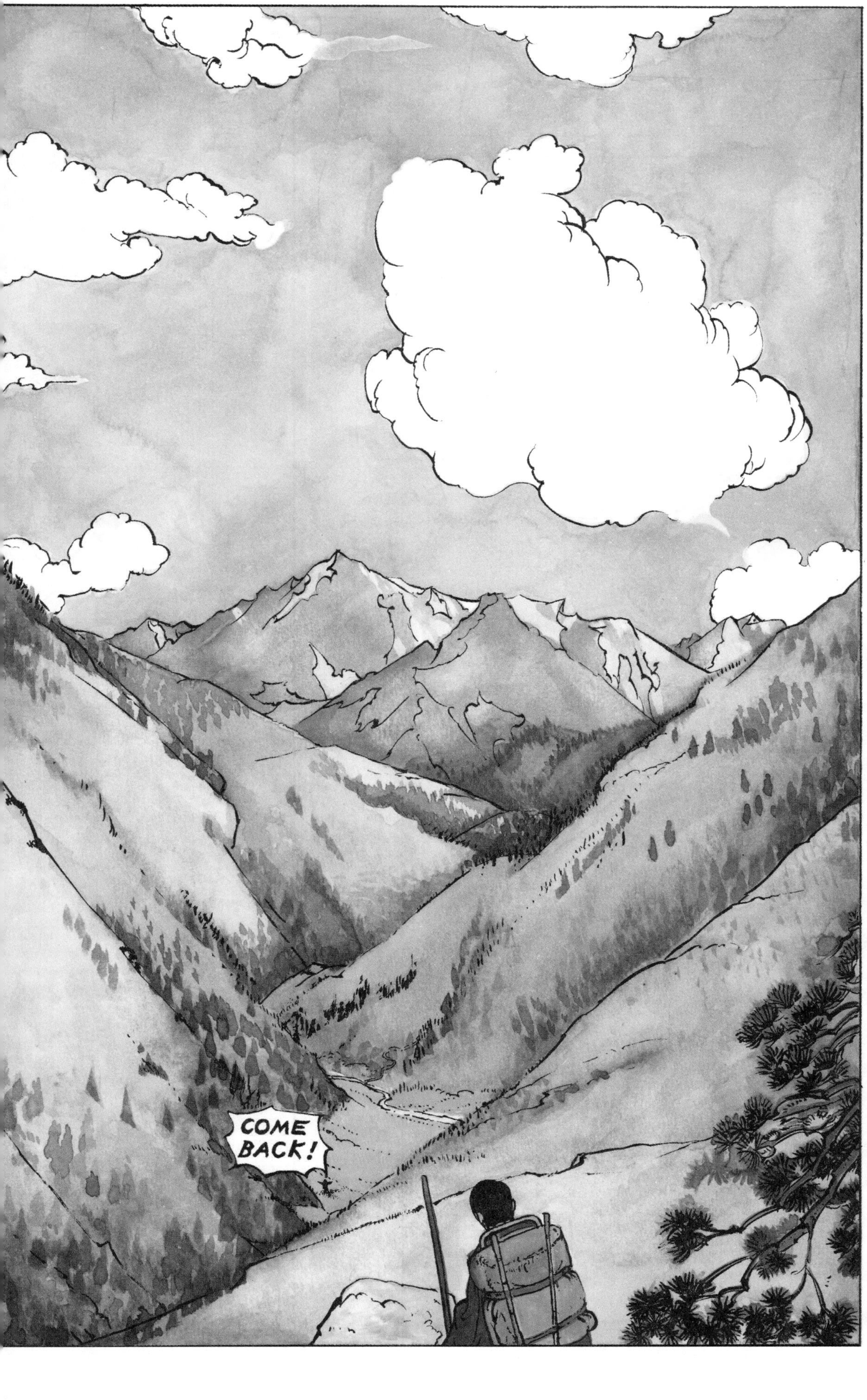
COME BACK!

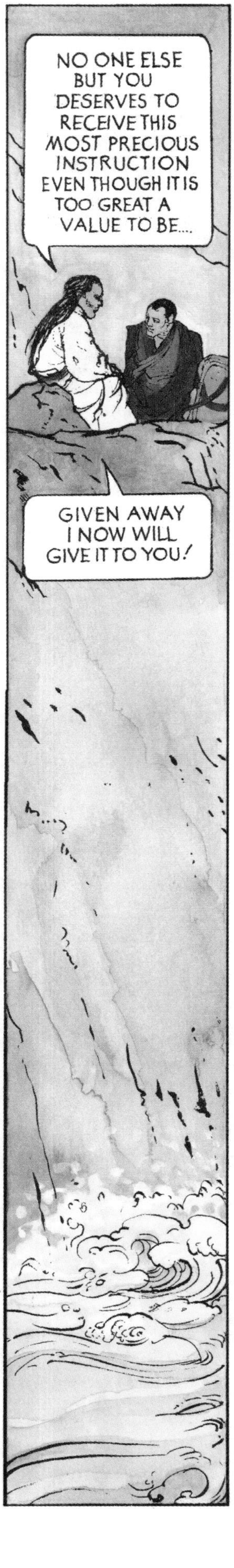
NO ONE ELSE BUT YOU DESERVES TO RECEIVE THIS MOST PRECIOUS INSTRUCTION EVEN THOUGH IT IS TOO GREAT A VALUE TO BE....
GIVEN AWAY I NOW WILL GIVE IT TO YOU!

CHERISH THIS TEACHING AND NEVER WASTE IT!

NOW LOOK!

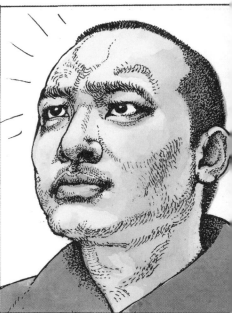

MILAREPA LIFTED THE BACK OF HIS ROBE, REVEALING HIS BEHIND COVERED WITH LUMPS OF HARD CALLUS LIKE THE HOOVES OF AN ANIMAL.

THIS IS DUE TO HAVING

SAT FOR SO LONG

ON STONY GROUND

WITHOUT CUSHION.

YOU NEED SUCH AN EFFORT.

THIS IS THE ESSENCE AND THE

MOST PROFOUND TEACHING IN BUDDHISM: PRACTICE!

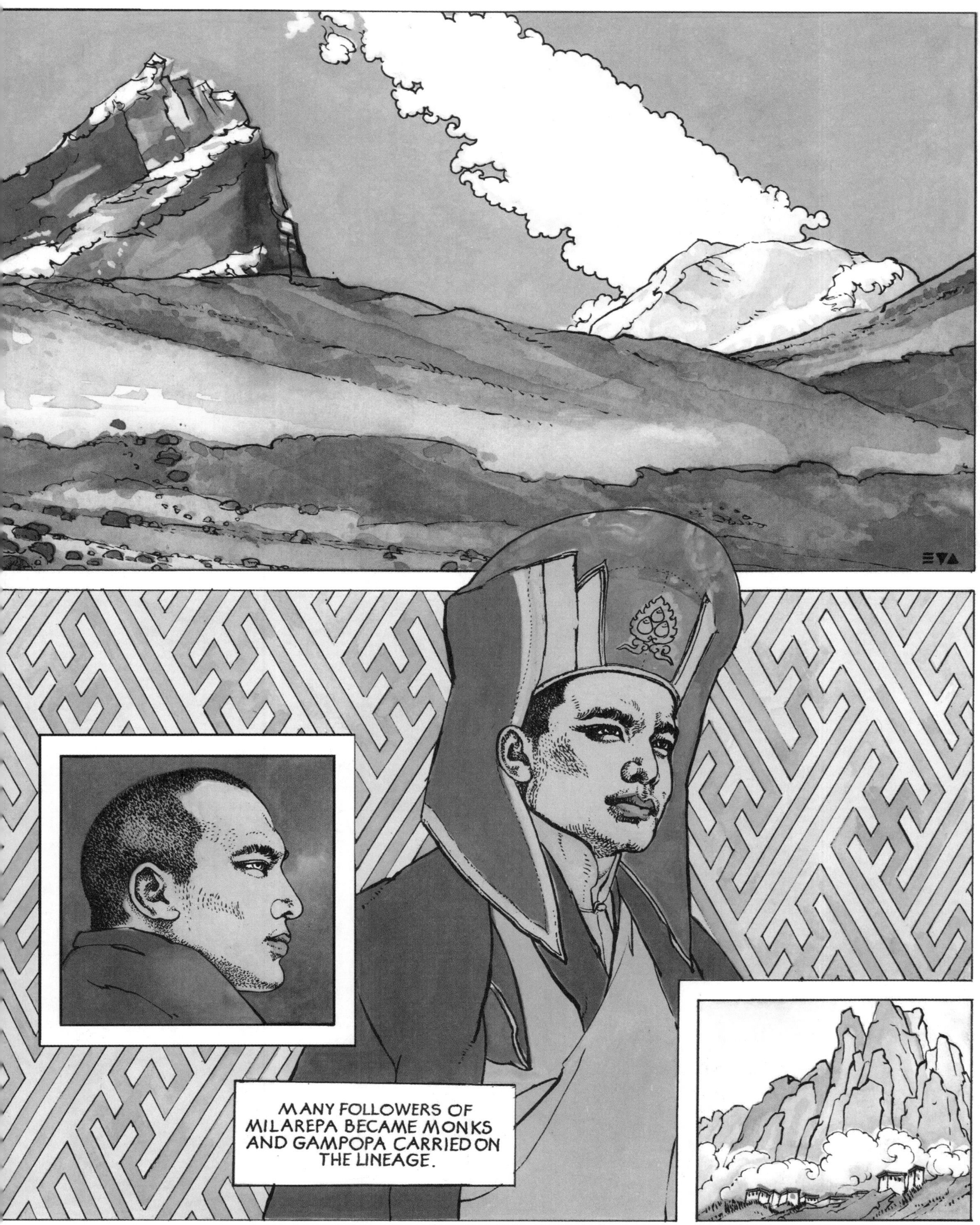
EVA
MANY FOLLOWERS OF MILAREPA BECAME MONKS AND GAMPOPA CARRIED ON THE LINEAGE.

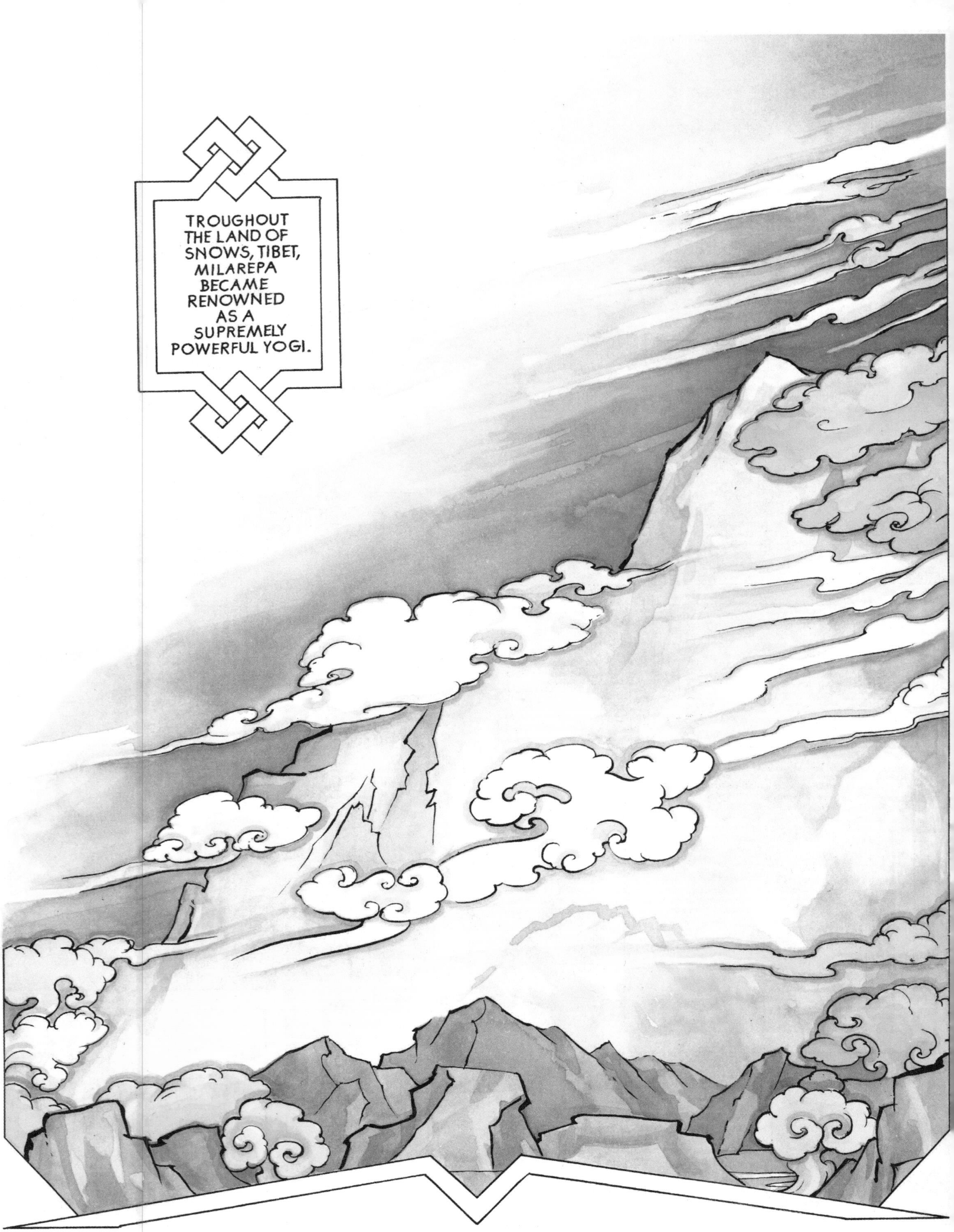
TROUGHOUT THE LAND OF SNOWS, TIBET, MILAREPA BECAME RENOWNED AS A SUPREMELY POWERFUL YOGI.

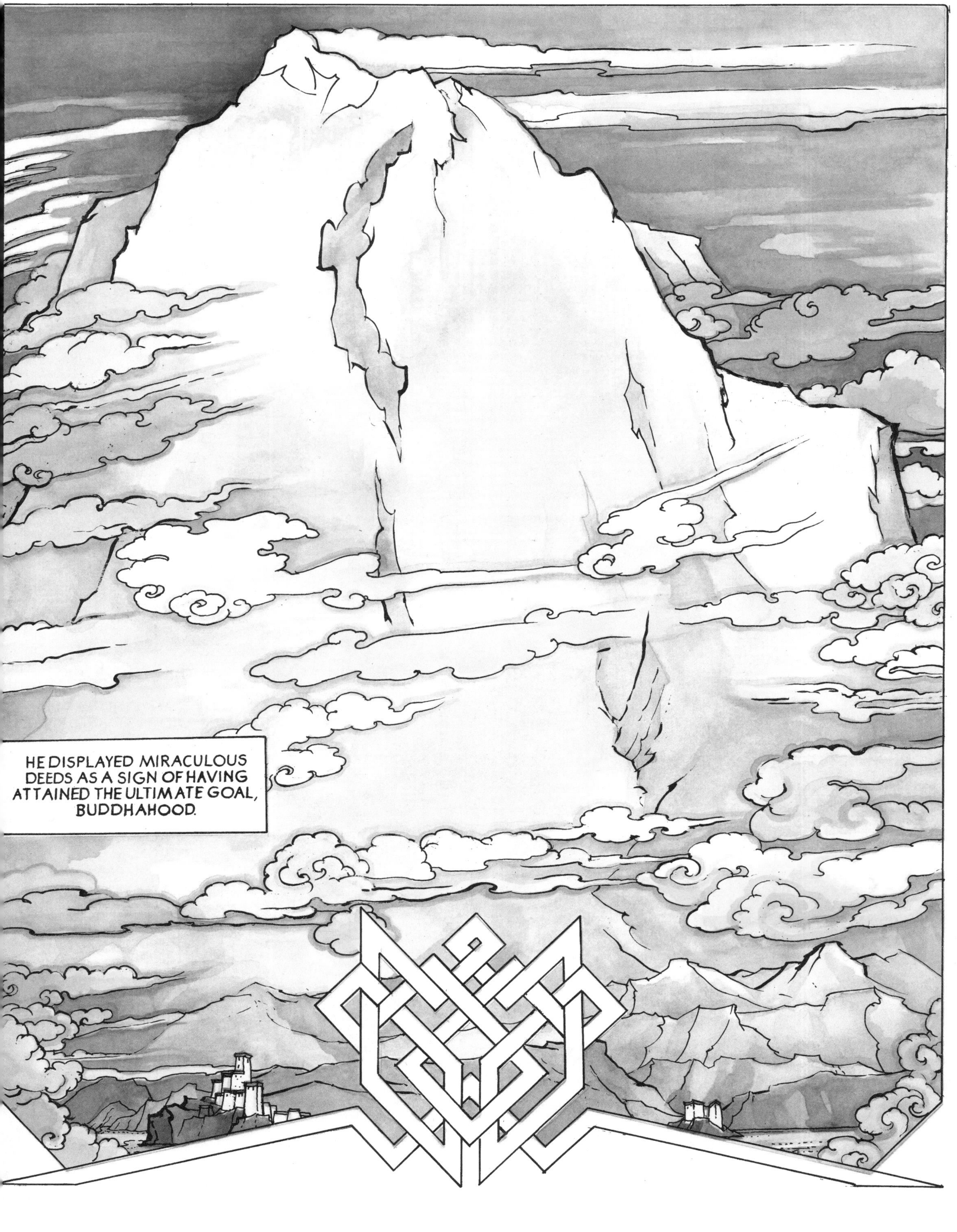
HE DISPLAYED MIRACULOUS DEEDS AS A SIGN OF HAVING ATTAINED THE ULTIMATE GOAL, BUDDHAHOOD.

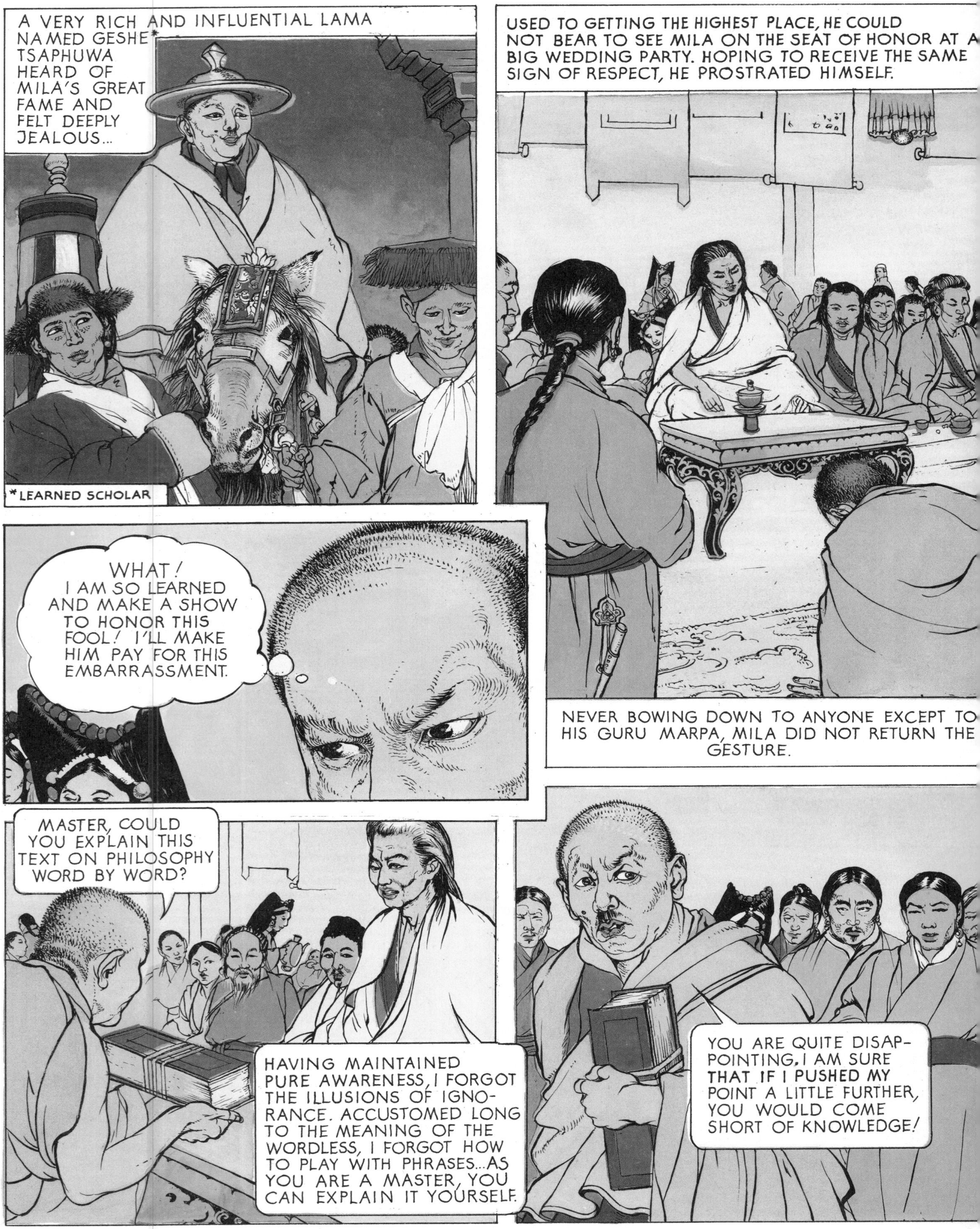
A VERY RICH AND INFLUENTIAL LAMA NAMED GESHE* TSAPHUWA HEARD OF MILA'S GREAT FAME AND FELT DEEPLY JEALOUS...
*LEARNED SCHOLAR
USED TO GETTING THE HIGHEST PLACE, HE COULD NOT BEAR TO SEE MILA ON THE SEAT OF HONOR AT A BIG WEDDING PARTY. HOPING TO RECEIVE THE SAME SIGN OF RESPECT, HE PROSTRATED HIMSELF.
NEVER BOWING DOWN TO ANYONE EXCEPT TO HIS GURU MARPA, MILA DID NOT RETURN THE GESTURE.
WHAT! I AM SO LEARNED AND MAKE A SHOW TO HONOR THIS FOOL! I'LL MAKE HIM PAY FOR THIS EMBARRASSMENT.
MASTER, COULD YOU EXPLAIN THIS TEXT ON PHILOSOPHY WORD BY WORD?
HAVING MAINTAINED PURE AWARENESS, I FORGOT THE ILLUSIONS OF IGNO-RANCE. ACCUSTOMED LONG TO THE MEANING OF THE WORDLESS, I FORGOT HOW TO PLAY WITH PHRASES...AS YOU ARE A MASTER, YOU CAN EXPLAIN IT YOURSELF.
YOU ARE QUITE DISAP-POINTING. I AM SURE THAT IF I PUSHED MY POINT A LITTLE FURTHER, YOU WOULD COME SHORT OF KNOWLEDGE!

MASTER GESHE, YOU SHOULD SHUT UP NOW, YOU CANNOT MEASURE UP TO THE MASTER IN ANY WAY!

THIS HUMILIATION IS UNBEARABLE! THE MAN IS A CORRUPTOR OF THE PURE TEACHINGS. I MUST PUT AN END TO THIS!

THAT'LL DO IT.

MIXING POISON IN A DISH WITH YOGHURT, HE CALLED HIS CONCUBINE....

THIS TURQUOISE IS FOR YOU, IF YOU TAKE THIS DISH TO MILAREPA. THERE'S POISON IN IT.

BRING IT BACK LATER, THEN I'LL DRINK IT.

KNOWING HIS TIME HAD COME, EVEN IF HE DID NOT TAKE THE POISON, AND THAT THE REWARD WOULD NOT BE GIVEN TO THE WOMAN AFTERWARDS...

HE IS CLAIRVOYANT! HE SUSPECTED ME AND DID NOT DRINK IT.

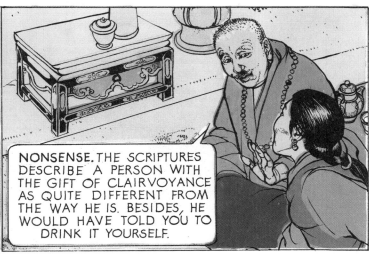

NONSENSE. THE SCRIPTURES DESCRIBE A PERSON WITH THE GIFT OF CLAIRVOYANCE AS QUITE DIFFERENT FROM THE WAY HE IS. BESIDES, HE WOULD HAVE TOLD YOU TO DRINK IT YOURSELF.

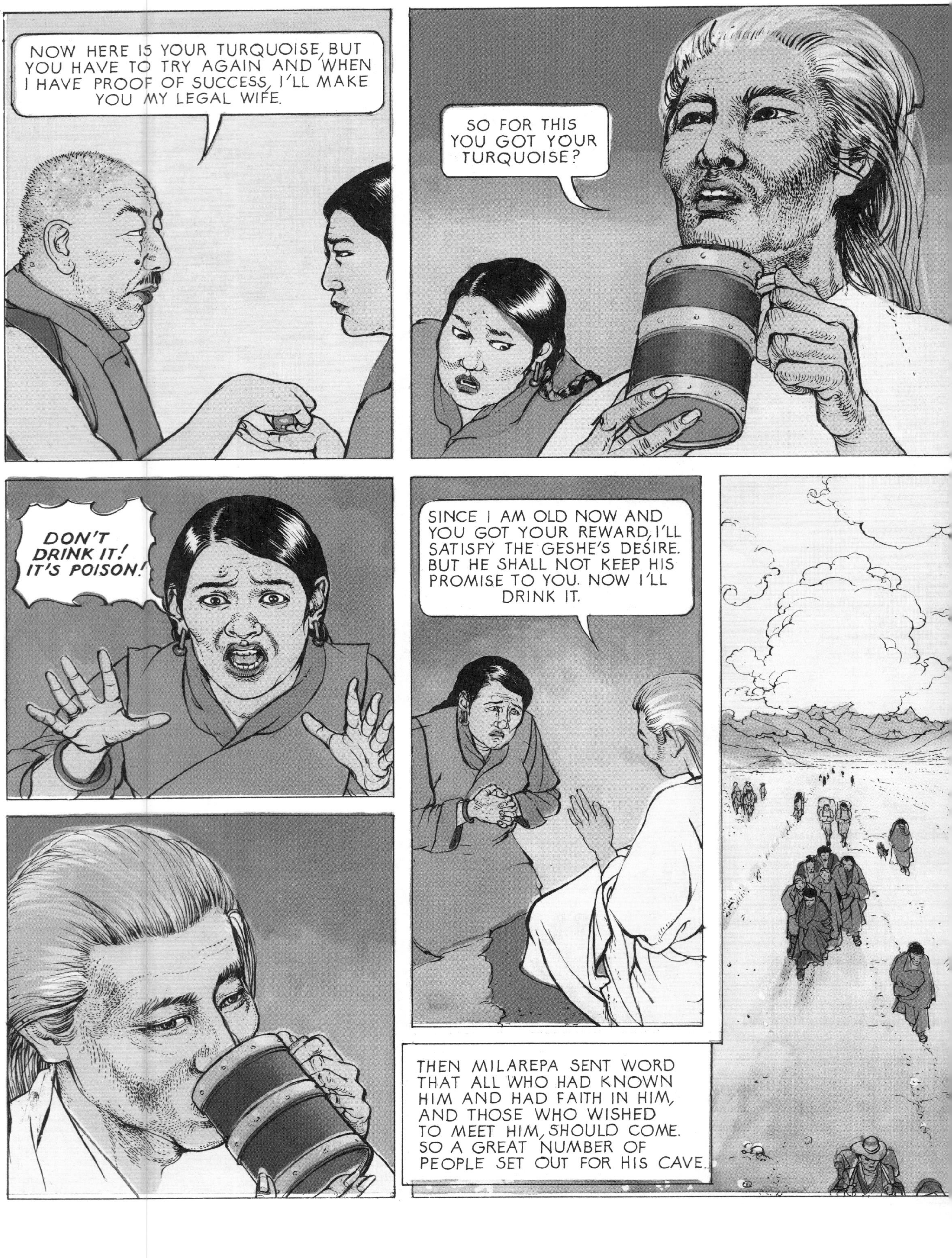
NOW HERE IS YOUR TURQUOISE, BUT YOU HAVE TO TRY AGAIN AND WHEN I HAVE PROOF OF SUCCESS, I'LL MAKE YOU MY LEGAL WIFE.
SO FOR THIS YOU GOT YOUR TURQUOISE?
DON'T DRINK IT! IT'S POISON!
SINCE I AM OLD NOW AND YOU GOT YOUR REWARD, I'LL SATISFY THE GESHE'S DESIRE. BUT HE SHALL NOT KEEP HIS PROMISE TO YOU. NOW I'LL DRINK IT.
THEN MILAREPA SENT WORD THAT ALL WHO HAD KNOWN HIM AND HAD FAITH IN HIM, AND THOSE WHO WISHED TO MEET HIM, SHOULD COME. SO A GREAT NUMBER OF PEOPLE SET OUT FOR HIS CAVE.

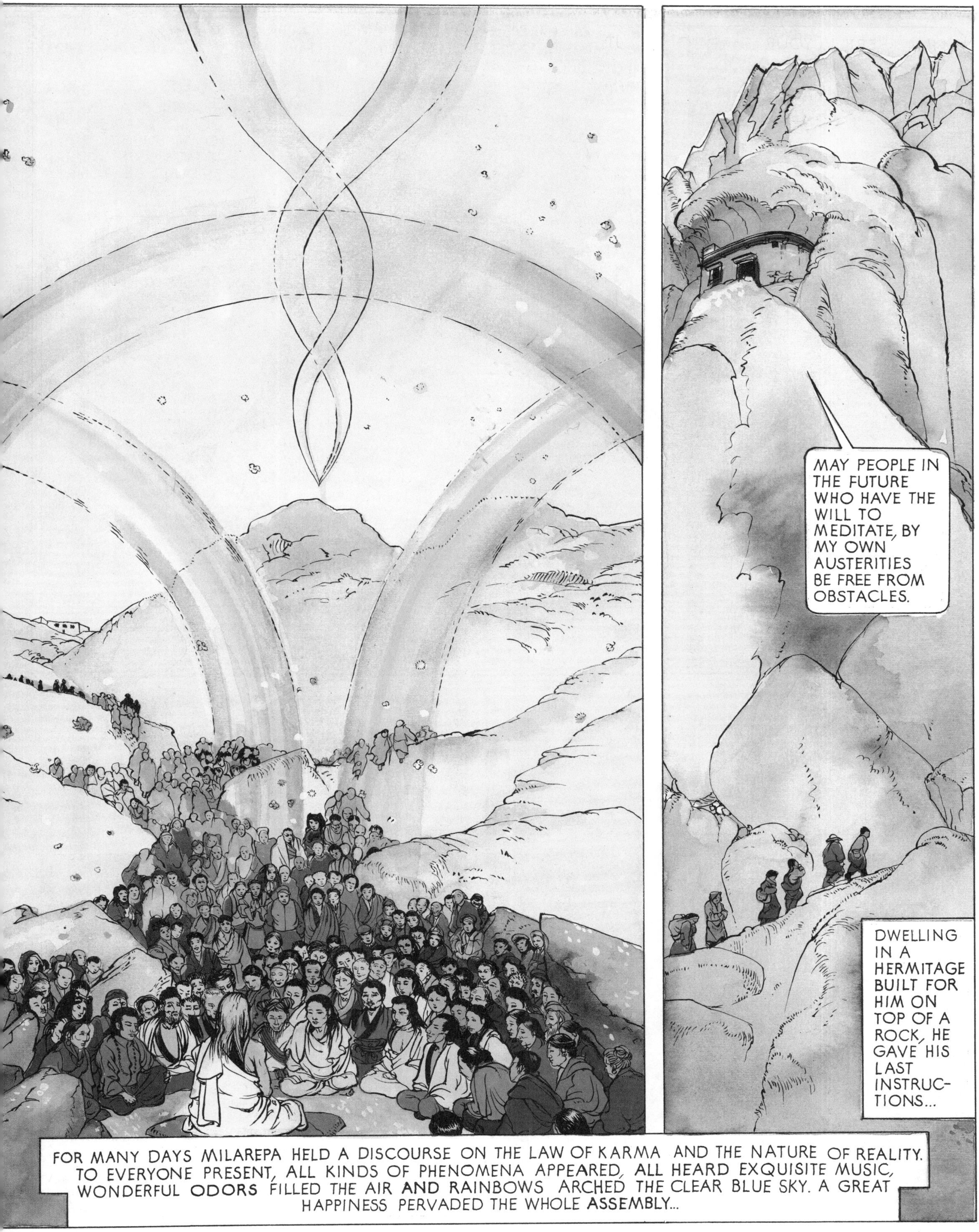
FOR MANY DAYS MILAREPA HELD A DISCOURSE ON THE LAW OF KARMA AND THE NATURE OF REALITY. TO EVERYONE PRESENT, ALL KINDS OF PHENOMENA APPEARED, ALL HEARD EXQUISITE MUSIC, WONDERFUL ODORS FILLED THE AIR AND RAINBOWS ARCHED THE CLEAR BLUE SKY. A GREAT HAPPINESS PERVADED THE WHOLE ASSEMBLY...
DWELLING IN A HERMITAGE BUILT FOR HIM ON TOP OF A ROCK, HE GAVE HIS LAST INSTRUC-TIONS...
MAY PEOPLE IN THE FUTURE WHO HAVE THE WILL TO MEDITATE, BY MY OWN AUSTERITIES BE FREE FROM OBSTACLES.

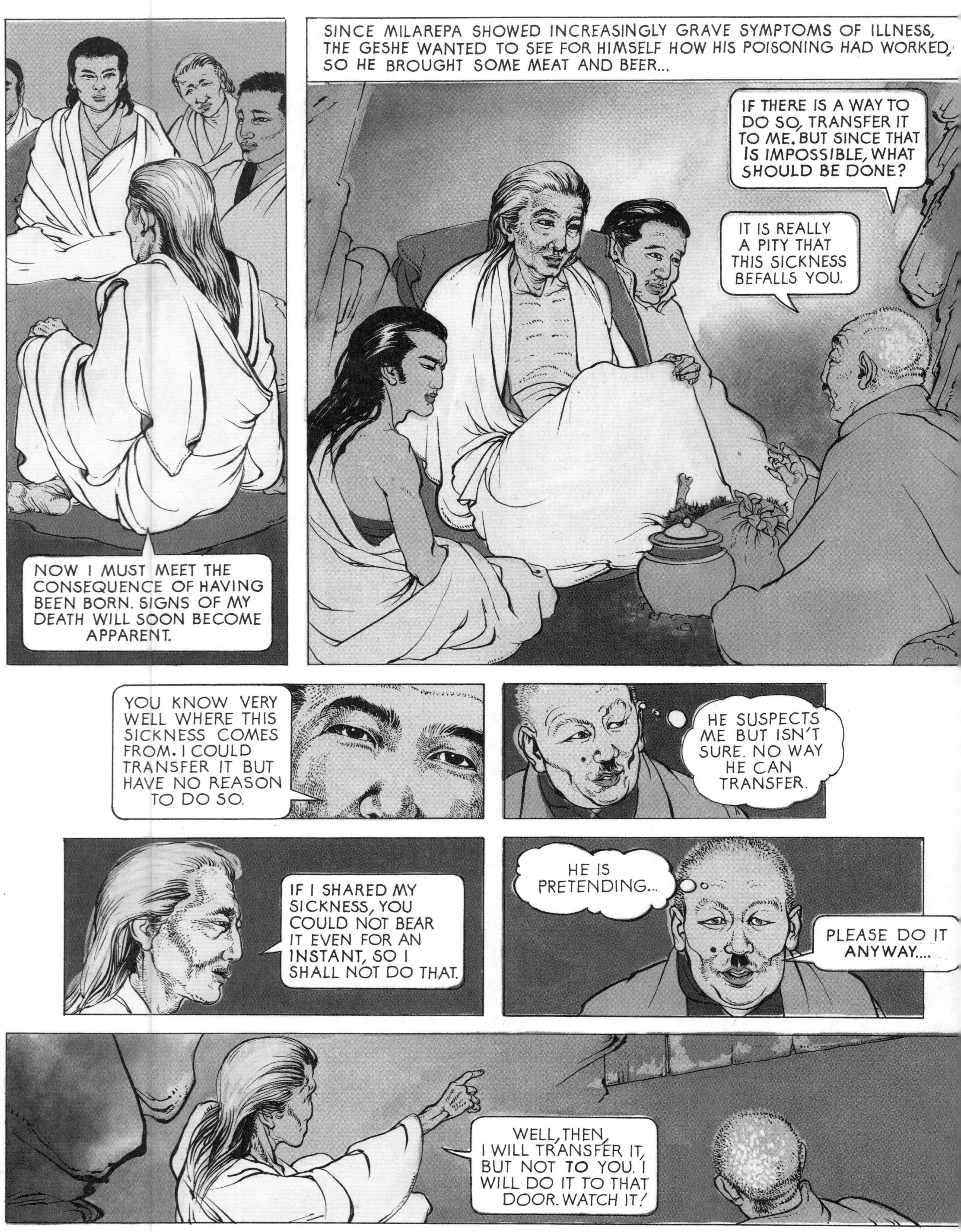
NOW I MUST MEET THE CONSEQUENCE OF HAVING BEEN BORN. SIGNS OF MY DEATH WILL SOON BECOME APPARENT.
SINCE MILAREPA SHOWED INCREASINGLY GRAVE SYMPTOMS OF ILLNESS, THE GESHE WANTED TO SEE FOR HIMSELF HOW HIS POISONING HAD WORKED, SO HE BROUGHT SOME MEAT AND BEER...
IT IS REALLY A PITY THAT THIS SICKNESS BEFALLS YOU.
IF THERE IS A WAY TO DO SO, TRANSFER IT TO ME. BUT SINCE THAT IS IMPOSSIBLE, WHAT SHOULD BE DONE?
YOU KNOW VERY WELL WHERE THIS SICKNESS COMES FROM. I COULD TRANSFER IT BUT HAVE NO REASON TO DO SO.
HE SUSPECTS ME BUT ISN'T SURE. NO WAY HE CAN TRANSFER.
IF I SHARED MY SICKNESS, YOU COULD NOT BEAR IT EVEN FOR AN INSTANT, SO I SHALL NOT DO THAT.
HE IS PRETENDING...
PLEASE DO IT ANYWAY....
WELL, THEN, I WILL TRANSFER IT, BUT NOT TO YOU. I WILL DO IT TO THAT DOOR. WATCH IT!

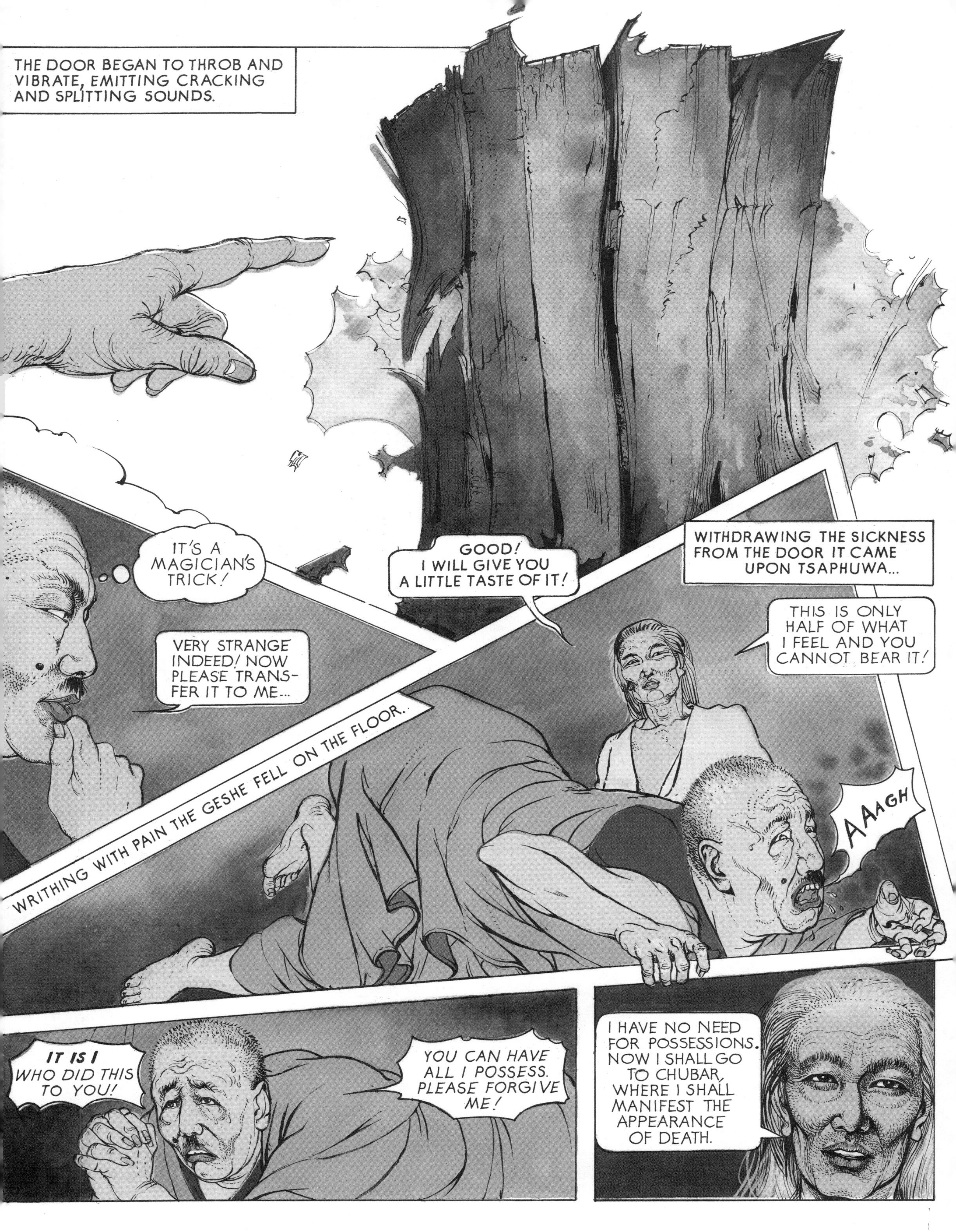
THE DOOR BEGAN TO THROB AND VIBRATE, EMITTING CRACKING AND SPLITTING SOUNDS.
IT'S A MAGICIAN'S TRICK!
VERY STRANGE INDEED! NOW PLEASE TRANSFER IT TO ME...
GOOD! I WILL GIVE YOU A LITTLE TASTE OF IT!
WITHDRAWING THE SICKNESS FROM THE DOOR IT CAME UPON TSAPHUWA...
THIS IS ONLY HALF OF WHAT I FEEL AND YOU CANNOT BEAR IT!
WRITHING WITH PAIN THE GESHE FELL ON THE FLOOR.
AAAGH
IT IS I WHO DID THIS TO YOU!
YOU CAN HAVE ALL I POSSESS. PLEASE FORGIVE ME!
I HAVE NO NEED FOR POSSESSIONS. NOW I SHALL GO TO CHUBAR, WHERE I SHALL MANIFEST THE APPEARANCE OF DEATH.

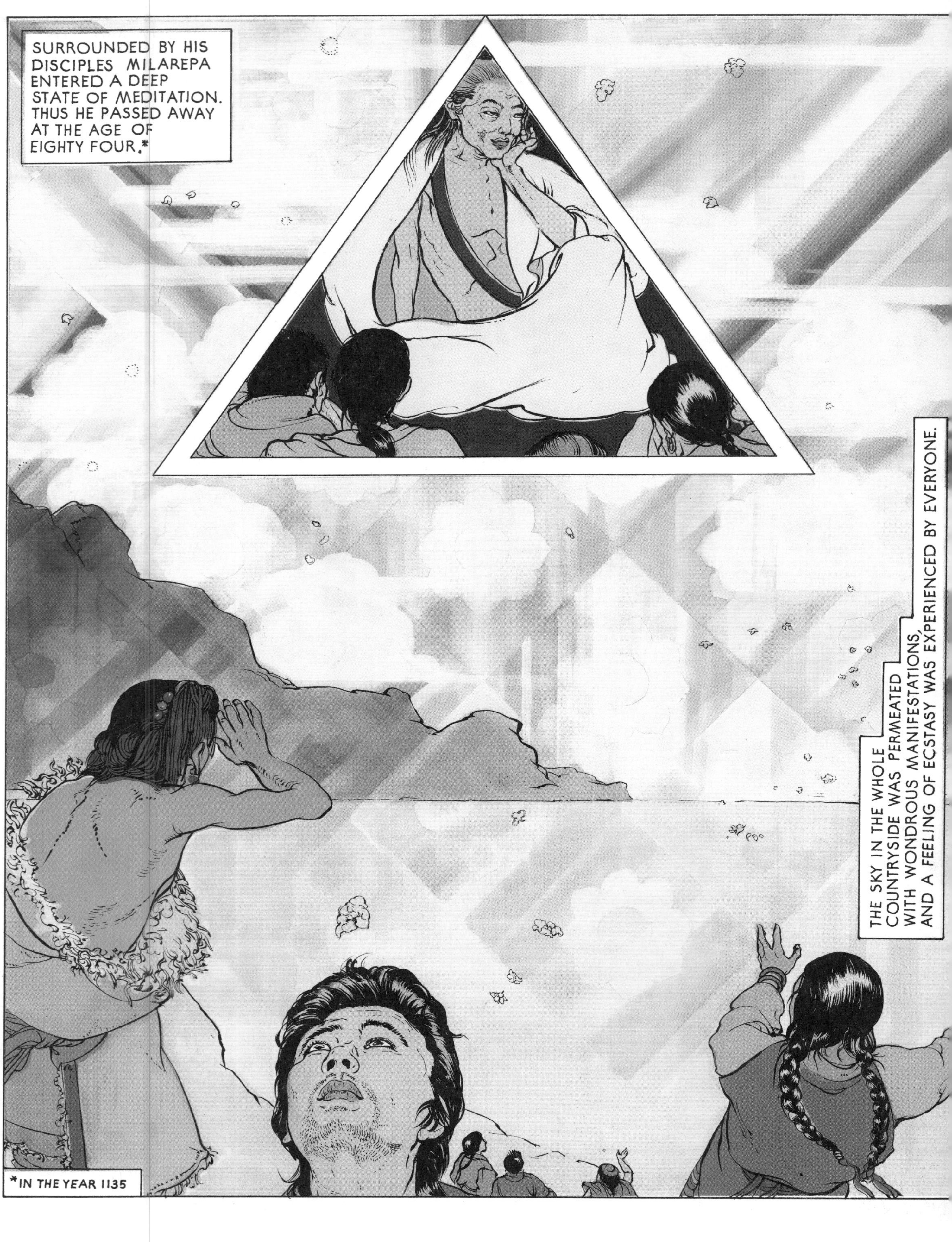
SURROUNDED BY HIS DISCIPLES MILAREPA ENTERED A DEEP STATE OF MEDITATION. THUS HE PASSED AWAY AT THE AGE OF EIGHTY FOUR.*
THE SKY IN THE WHOLE COUNTRYSIDE WAS PERMEATED WITH WONDROUS MANIFESTATIONS, AND A FEELING OF ECSTASY WAS EXPERIENCED BY EVERYONE.
*IN THE YEAR 1135

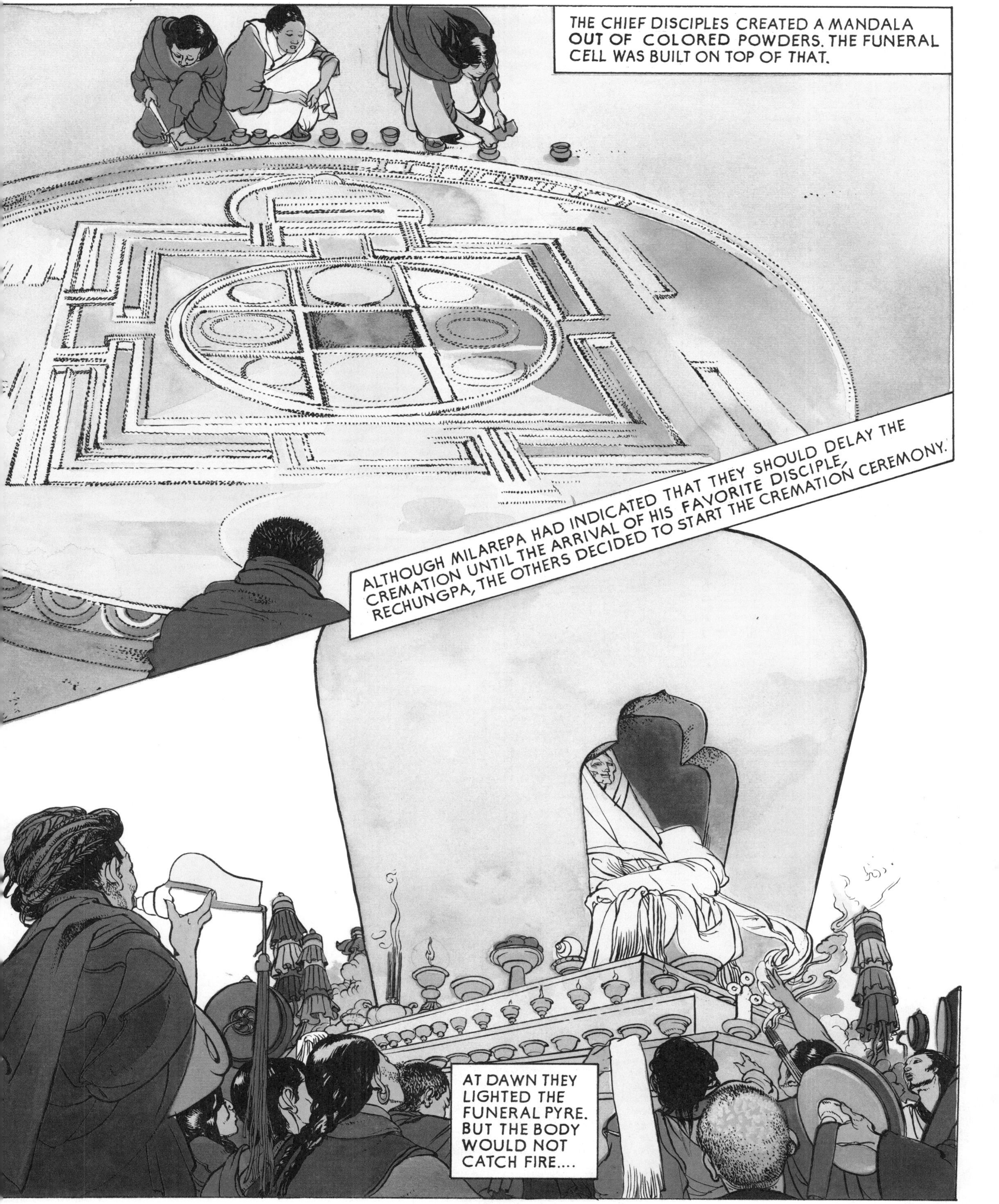
THE CHIEF DISCIPLES CREATED A MANDALA OUT OF COLORED POWDERS. THE FUNERAL CELL WAS BUILT ON TOP OF THAT.
ALTHOUGH MILAREPA HAD INDICATED THAT THEY SHOULD DELAY THE CREMATION UNTIL THE ARRIVAL OF HIS FAVORITE DISCIPLE, RECHUNGPA, THE OTHERS DECIDED TO START THE CREMATION CEREMONY.
AT DAWN THEY LIGHTED THE FUNERAL PYRE. BUT THE BODY WOULD NOT CATCH FIRE....

RECHUNGPA FINALLY ARRIVED. NOT KNOWING WHO HE WAS, SOME OF THE MOST RECENTLY ACCEPTED DISCIPLES STOPPED AND PREVENTED HIM FROM GOING TOWARD THE BODY.

OH LAMA! I AM PREVENTED FROM SEEING YOUR FACE FOR THE LAST TIME!

PLEASE HAVE MERCY ON ME...

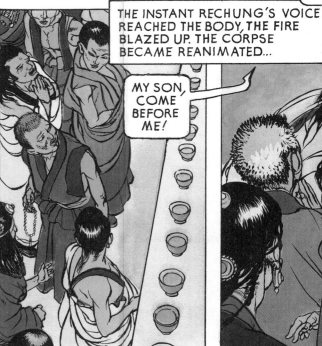

MY SON, COME BEFORE ME!

MILAREPA'S DISEMBODIED VOICE WAS HEARD BY ALL...

O RECHUNG, DEAREST TO MY HEART. ABANDON CONCEPTS, REALIZE ALL-ENCOMPASSING EMPTINESS, AND DISSOLVE ALL DUALITY! THIS IS MY VERY LAST WILL.

LISTEN TO THIS OLD MAN'S FINAL WORDS...

THE INSTANT RECHUNG'S VOICE REACHED THE BODY, THE FIRE BLAZED UP. THE CORPSE BECAME REANIMATED...

THE EVENING HAD SET IN WHEN THE FUNERAL PYRE HAD BURNT OUT. EXPECTING WONDROUS RELICS, ALL WENT TO SLEEP NEXT TO IT. IN THE EARLY DAWN RECHUNGPA DREAMT OF DAKINIS* CARRYING AWAY A SPHERE OF LIGHT. WAKING THE OTHERS UP, THEY LOOKED INTO THE CREMATION HOUSE...

* KEEPERS OF WISDOM.

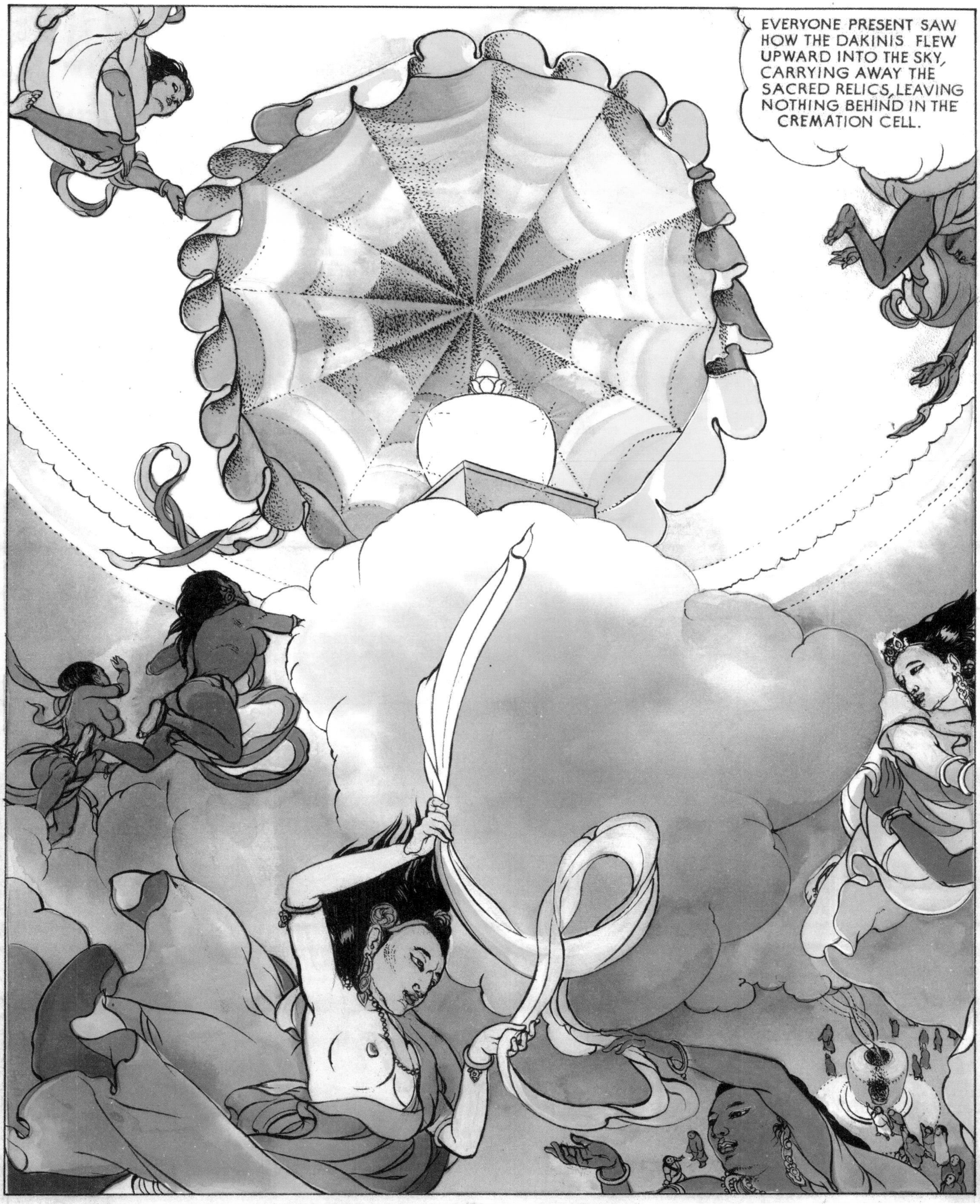
EVERYONE PRESENT SAW HOW THE DAKINIS FLEW UPWARD INTO THE SKY, CARRYING AWAY THE SACRED RELICS, LEAVING NOTHING BEHIND IN THE CREMATION CELL.

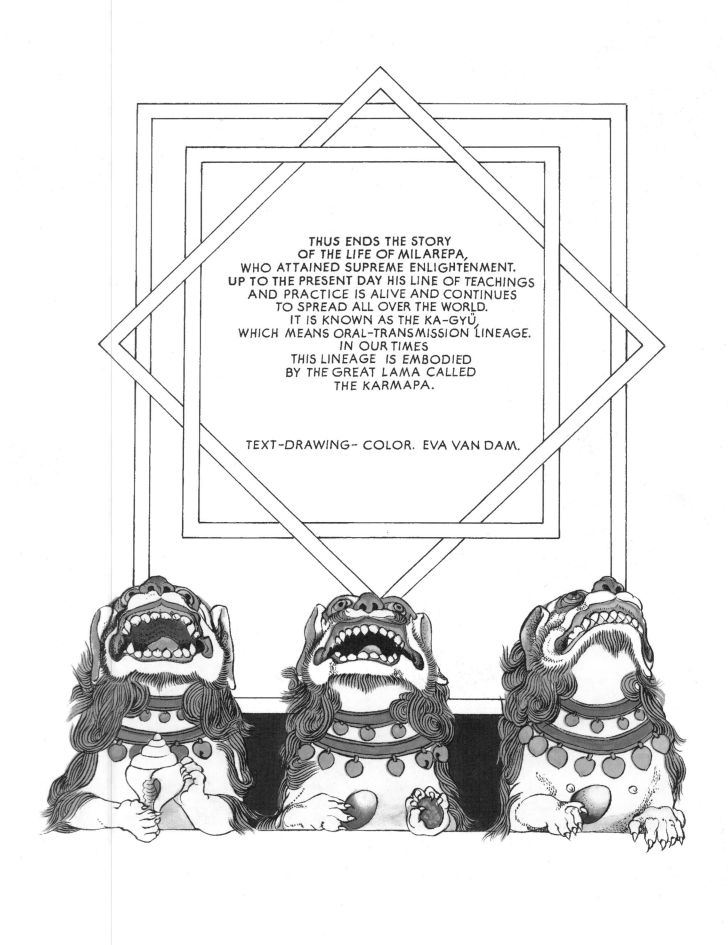

THUS ENDS THE STORY
OF THE LIFE OF MILAREPA,
WHO ATTAINED SUPREME ENLIGHTENMENT.
UP TO THE PRESENT DAY HIS LINE OF TEACHINGS
AND PRACTICE IS ALIVE AND CONTINUES
TO SPREAD ALL OVER THE WORLD.
IT IS KNOWN AS THE KA-GYÜ,
WHICH MEANS ORAL-TRANSMISSION LINEAGE.
IN OUR TIMES
THIS LINEAGE IS EMBODIED
BY THE GREAT LAMA CALLED
THE KARMAPA.

TEXT-DRAWING- COLOR. EVA VAN DAM.